Québec and the Heritage of Franco-America

Edited by

Iwan Morgan and Philip Davies

INSTITUTE FOR THE STUDY OF THE
AMERICAS

UNIVERSITY OF LONDON · SCHOOL OF ADVANCED STUDY

British Library Cataloguing-in-Publication Data
A catalogue record for this book is available from the British Library

ISBN 978 1 900039 98 7

INSTITUTE FOR THE STUDY OF THE
A M E R I C A S
UNIVERSITY OF LONDON · SCHOOL OF ADVANCED STUDY

Institute for the Study of the Americas
School of Advanced Study
University of London
Senate House
London WC1E 7HU

Telephone: 020 7862 8870
Fax: 020 7862 8886

Email: americas@sas.ac.uk
Web: www.americas.sas.ac.uk

Contents

Notes on Contributors

Barry Jean Ancelet is Granger and Debaillon/BORSF Endowed [Board of Regents Support Fund] Professor of Francophone Studies and Folklore at the University of Louisiana at Lafayette. A renowned authority on Louisiana's Cajun and Creole cultures and languages, he has published extensively in this field, including *One Generation at a Time: Biography of a Cajun and Creole Music Festival* (2007), *Cajun and Creole Music Makers* (1984/1999), *Cajun Country* (1991), *Cajun Music: Origins and Development* (1989) and *Cajun and Creole Folktales* (1994). He has also contributed to numerous documentary films, including *Against the Tide* (2001), *Dance for a Chicken: The Cajun Country Mardi Gras* (1993) and *J'ai été au bal: the Cajun and Zydeco music of Louisiana* (1989), as well as a number of radio programmes on Louisiana French culture. He serves as director of the annual Festival de Musique Acadienne component of Festivals Acadiens and hosts the 'Rendez-vous des Cajuns,' a weekly live radio show from the Liberty Theater in Eunice, Louisiana. He is a Chevalier in France's Palmes Académiques and in France's Ordre des Arts et des Lettres, a member of Québec's Ordre des Francophones d'Amérique and a Fellow of the American Folklore Society.

Lise Bissonnette, writer and journalist, was president and director of the Bibliothèque et Archives Nationales du Québec from 1998 to 2009. She was educated at the University of Montréal and undertook doctoral studies at the University of Strasbourg and the Ecole Pratique des Hautes Etudes. In 1974 she started as a journalist at *Le Devoir*, eventually becoming its editor-in-chief from 1990–8. Among her many honours, she is an Officer of the National Order of Québec and a holder of France's Légion d'Honneur.

Bill Marshall is Professor of Comparative Literary and Cultural Studies at the University of Stirling, having previously worked at Glasgow and Southampton universities. He is the author of *Victor Serge: The Uses of Dissent* (1992), *Guy Hocquenghem* (1996), *Quebec National Cinema* (2001) and most recently, *André Téchiné* (2007), in the French Film Directors series from Manchester University Press. Among the numerous works he has edited are: *Musicals: Hollywood and Beyond* (2000); *Montreal-Glasgow* (2005); and the three-volume encyclopaedia *France and the Americas* (2005). His recently completed monograph entitled *The French Atlantic: Travels in Culture and History* is published by Liverpool University Press.

Jean Morisset has a PhD in Geography and Latin American Studies from the University of Liverpool and is currently an associate professor at the Université du Québec à Montréal. Born in Bellechasse-en-Canada on the shores of the Saint Lawrence River, he worked as a seaman on icebreakers during the 1960s and was part of a vast exploration programme in the High Arctic and the Mackenzie Valley in the Canadian Northwest Territories. He followed this with intensive field work in the Caribbean (he is part of the AfricAmericA Forum in Haiti), in Peru, Guatemala, Mexico and, for the last 25 years, in Brazil. But it is his work in land claims research throughout Canada and particularly with *Métis* issues (in the USA as well) that has developed his interest in Franco-America and Métis-America. He has recently participated in a book project to be released with the new feature film, *Before Tomorrow,* from Isuma Productions (Igloolik and Montréal).

Eric Waddell is Adjunct Professor at Université Laval and an Honorary Professor at the University of Sydney (Australia). Having earned his first degree at Oxford, he moved to Québec in the early 1960s to pursue his studies. His arrival coincided with the birth of a modern, secular society and polity, which precipitated his involvement in the ongoing debate on Québec's identity and destiny. Choosing to approach this from the francophone periphery (Newfoundland and Louisiana) rather than from the centre, he produced a number of path-breaking studies over the next 40 years. These include: *Le Québec et l'Amérique Française: Du Continent Perdu à l'Archipel Retrouvé* (1983, 2007); (with Jean Morisset) *Amériques* (2000); (with Dean Louder and Jean Morisset) *Vision et Visages de la Franco-Amérique* (2003); and *Franco-Amérique* (2008). As these titles indicate, his work signifies a desire to highlight a distinctively North American francophone experience as distinct from a projection of a European reality.

Eric Wauters is Professor of History at the Université du Havre. His research focuses upon writing and reading from the late 18th to the beginning of the 19th century. He is a member of the Canadian Association for the Study of Book Culture and presented papers at the Association's Second Annual Conference at York University in 2006 ('The Book in the City') and its third conference at the University of Saskatchewan in 2007 ('Books and the Making of Knowledge'). The text for the latter appears in *Papers of Bibliographical Society of Canada*, 45, no. 2. He collaborated on the *Dictionnaire de la Presse Française Pendant la Révolution, 1789–1799*, Gilles Feyel (ed.), 2005 and (with Catriona Seth of the University of Rouen) co-edited *Un Siècle de Journalisme Culturel en Normandie et dans les Autres Provinces, 1785–1885* and *La Normandie et le Monde Tropical, Trois Siècles de Relations (XIVe–début XIXe siècle)*.

INTRODUCTION
QUEBEC AND THE HERITAGE OF FRANCO-AMERICA

Iwan Morgan

This book is the outcome of a conference[1] held in the British Library to mark the 400th anniversary of the founding in 1608, by French explorer and navigator Samuel de Champlain, of the settlement that became the city of Québec. Co-organised by the British Library's Eccles Centre for American Studies and the University of London's Institute for the Study of the Americas, this event drew together scholars from Québec, Louisiana and France to explore the heritage of Franco-America that developed in the centuries following Québec's founding. It received enthusiastic support from the Québec Office, the United States Embassy, the French Embassy and the Canadian High Commission in London, without whose financial support the venture could never have become a reality. The six essays in this study highlight the themes and issues explored in the conference.

The essays are gathered together under the volume title, *Québec and the Heritage of Franco-America*. It is an important editorial task to establish at the outset what is meant by *heritage* and *Franco-America* in the scholarship of the contributors as both terms are contestable and capable of misunderstanding.

One way of interpreting heritage in relation to Québec's 400th anniversary might be to focus on the survival of a minority culture in North America as a relic of a French empire that held temporary sway over a part of this continent from 1607 to 1759. Nothing could be further from the intent of the contributors to this study. In their construct, Québec is at the centre of a vibrant Franco-American heritage that is durable and viable thanks to the instrumentalities of time (history), place (geography) and identity (culture).

Indeed, fundamental to the scholarship in this volume is that heritage in the context of Franco-America is not remembrance of a lost French culture, but rather the shaping influence of an identity that was neither French nor American, but one that amalgamated unique characteristics from both cultures.

---

1   'Québec, Louisiana and the French Heritage of North America', 5 March, 2007.

In this regard, the founding of Québec and the corollary establishment of New France was a beginning, but the Conquest of 1759 (or its ratification in the 1763 Treaty of Paris) did not mark the end point of the formative elements of Franco-America's heritage. In reality, these continued to grow and develop over the next two and a half centuries, with the movement over large swathes of North America of people tracing their lineage to Québec and carrying their Franco-American culture with them. In other words, time, place and identity were fluid and empowering rather than fixed and restraining elements in the making of their heritage.

The use of the term, Franco-America, also has significance in this regard. While our volume marks the 400th anniversary of the founding of Québec, our concern is to analyse the significance of this not only for the latter-day city and province as a francophone enclave within Canada, but also for the centrifugal spread of an identity far beyond the provincial borders. It might have been feasible to use the term *Canadien* heritage instead, since that was the self-description broadly used by the inhabitants of Québec by the time of the Conquest and certainly in the post-Conquest century. However, this would have implied geographical limits to the *Canadien* heritage that did not exist in reality.

Another possibility would have been to use the term French North America. In fact this was employed in the title of the actual conference on which the volume was based, but the presentations and the resultant essays cast doubt on its utility in this context. Firstly, it implies a hegemonic culture, but the geographical expansion over time of an identity initially implanted in Québec was the very opposite of this, in marked contrast to the Anglo-American model. Moreover, the term was misleading because, language apart, the fundamentals of the American continent's francophone culture are not French. Lastly, it bespeaks of something that is rooted in one well-defined space, by implication Québec, but this is wholly at variance with reality. The term Franco-American, in contrast, allows us to get closer to understanding the heritage that developed initially out of Québec's founding, but was not confined over time to the modern geographical limits of the political entity of that name. It also conveys a sense of *destiny* as well as heritage. Thanks to their particular history, those who might be termed Franco-Americans shared a *métis* culture that had francophone components and American ones, but was in essence a uniquely French Native American entity. However, the term should not be seen as correlating to the hyphenated definition of identity that we are accustomed to employing with regard to racial and ethnic groups in the United States (US). It entails more than the creation of a sub-identity that is within and fundamentally part of the dominant culture of a nation-state. Franco-American identity exists both within and beyond the boundaries of

Québec as it is a construct signifying a culture that extends beyond political and administrative boundaries rather than a means of explaining difference inside these limits.

It is within this interpretive framework that this volume marks the 400th anniversary of the founding of Québec and the significance of this for the modern Franco-American heritage. The six essays in the following pages deal with these complex and multi-faceted issues in fascinating inter-disciplinary detail that draws on the scholarship of history, geography, literature, language and culture.

Eric Waddell establishes many of the book's key themes in 'Québec and the Continental North American Experience'. In his view, the fact of being *born in America* rather than being an *immigrant to America* is the key to the distinctive linguistic and cultural identity of Franco-Americans. Theirs was a culture that spread far and wide across North America and penetrated well into the Anglo part of the continent (including the modern US) in the two centuries after the conquest. However, the continental dimensions of this identity ultimately gave way in Québec's 'Quiet Revolution' of the 1960s to a provincial one and its corollary nationalism. Waddell's essay advocates the rediscovery of the broader geographical dimensions of Franco-America lest critical elements of Québec's heritage become seen as something alien and unknown — to the detriment of its own sense of being. Not the least of the many fascinating elements of his essay is its exploration of how literary figures of Franco-America, such as Jack Kerouac and Gabrielle Roy, made the greatest effort — even though only partially successful — to unify the centrifugal continental experience into an overarching narrative.

Jean Morisset further explores the continual spread of Franco-American culture in 'The Head of this River is Unknown! ... Between *Truchement* and *Métissage*: The *Canadien's trajectoire* in the formation of the Americas'. In his view, Québec's 400th anniversary makes it incumbent to understand that the *Canadien* quest for identity encompasses a diversified *Métis* Canadian America, which goes beyond the idea of both a European French and a British America because it is, through origin and destiny, a mixed product of widespread francophone travels through a Native North America in its geographic totality. According to Morisset, *Canadien* America remained present in the history of the continent after 1759, carried forward not only by people tracing their lineage to the land that was once New France but also those from other parts of the francophone New World, notably Louisiana and the Caribbean. Urging scholars to trace this Franco-American identity from sources other than formal records that are the documentation of empire, he engages in a fascinating exploration of maps, stories and place names for this purpose.

Bill Marshall, in 'The Spaces of Québec City', employs the provincial capital's identity investments as a metaphor for what it means to be Franco-

American. In his assessment, the concentric circles that characterise its spatial configurations symbolise the transformation of not only a territory but also a culture. On this basis, he examines the evolution of Québec City's symbolism within Franco-America through four stages of its development: origin, port, and fortress (1607 to circa 1800); topography, hierarchy and power (late 18th to mid 19th centuries); its differentiation from Montréal (mid 19th to mid 20th centuries); and heritage and tourism (late 20th century to the present). According to Marshall, questions of topography and power, homogenisation and peripheralisation interlink with those of port and fortress to express a rhythm of opening and closing in Québec's history that is so different to Montréal's. In an insightful final section, he shows how the interchange between *ouverture* and *chambranle* finds strongest expression in the relationship between heritage (memory and identity) and tourism (the world's view of the city) that dominates Québec's modern space.

Eric Wauters, in 'Forgetting France or Forging a New Nation: a stage in Canadian writing (1825–45)', analyses the way France and her affairs were represented in *Canadien* magazines and journals in the second quarter of the 19th century. The new ideas that influenced the French-speaking middle class in this critical era found expression in the writings of publishers and journalists. In generational terms, the latter were too young to be enthusiastic about the French Revolution but old enough to be disillusioned by the new and little-understood country that France had become. Moreover, they had grown up in a world where Britain was less an enemy than a protector. Now distant from France, the members of the *Canadien* intelligentsia sought to overcome the tensions they felt between nationalism and class consciousness, French-speaking and bilingualism, old France and Britain, reformism and conservatism, Europe and America. In time they looked to build a national identity through the instrumentality of an original national literature. As a consequence, Wauters argues, *Canadien* writers no longer imitated Europe but injected a new sense of being Franco-American into their writing.

Barry Jean Ancelet, in 'Québec, Acadia and Louisiana: the impact of reunions and gatherings', explores a triangular relationship that testifies to the breadth and depth of Franco-America. The Acadian-Cajun reunions initiated to mark the 200th anniversary of the *Grand Derangement* in 1955 served to reinforce francophone culture in Louisiana that had long been under pressure from Americanisation. The opening of a Québec official delegation in Louisiana in the late 1960s and the influx of a cohort of Québécois French-language teachers also proved significant in this regard. As Ancelet explains, the foundation of the Council for the Development of French in Louisiana grew out of this development and proved a significant promoter of Franco-American cultural interchange. Increasing Acadian-Louisiana interchanges from the 1970s to the present also had the effect of enhancing Acadian identity, graphically demonstrated by the formation in 1994 of the *Congrès Mondial Acadien*. The essay makes an important contribution to the collection in its demonstration of the growing vitality of modern Franco-America outside the geographical boundaries of Québec province.

Finally, **Lise Bissonnette** completes the collection with 'French North America: A journey through the Bibliothèque et Archives Nationales du Québec … and other interesting avenues'. Archival sources that are rich and varied in form are essential for the study and understanding of the heritage and identity of Franco-America. In a volume that has emphasised the importance of movement, Bissonnette leads us on a journey through the main collections relevant to this subject in Québec, the United Kingdom and France. At the end of the essay, she poses a number of questions as to the future direction of collections in an age when the Internet has expanded access to them. Should collections be federated to avoid duplication? If so, who should be in charge of coordinating efforts? What are the financial implications for large and small institutions? Will it be possible to take multinational inventories? Is the proliferation of tiny thematic sites beneficial or problematic? While an answer to these questions is beyond the scope of a single paper, the author offers us a glimpse of how modern technology is promoting the history of Franco-America at present and how it may do so in the future.

As the essays in this volume indicate, the Franco-American heritage that began with the founding of Québec 400 years ago is rich, varied and vibrant. It is an important field of study with which anyone with an interest in the Americas must aim to come to terms. Anglo-America, Hispanic America and Luso-America are conventionally accepted as the main divisions of the political and cultural geography of the mainland Americas. Nevertheless, all are identified with regional limits (though Hispanic immigration to the US is starting to change matters). In contrast, as this collection makes clear, Franco-America can stake its claim to being a significant part of what we understand to be the Americas, not only because it has thrived and grown over the course of four centuries, but also because it has transcended the regional and national boundaries of a continent. The celebration of the founding of Québec provides the right moment to explore why this event has had enduring significance far beyond the city and province of that name.

As befits a work of this nature, it is incumbent on the editors to acknowledge their debt to those whose help was essential to the making of this book. As indicated above, our various financial sponsors provided very necessary support to the venture. We also thank our contributors for making the book a reality. Lastly we thank our institutional colleagues for all their willing work on our behalf. In particular we acknowledge the help of Olga Jimenez and Karen

Perkins at the Institute for the Study of the Americas, Kare Bateman and Jean Petrovic of the Eccles Centre, and Emily Morrell of the University of London's School of Advanced Study publications unit. Particular thanks go to Valerie Hall, who oversaw the publication process from manuscript submission to book and whose command of French proved both masterly and indispensable to completion of the project.

1
QUÉBEC AND THE CONTINENTAL NORTH AMERICAN EXPERIENCE

Eric Waddell

La Nouvelle-France avait pris les proportions d'un empire. Lorsqu'elle
s'écroula, une autre immensité, en marge de ses frontières du sud et
de l'ouest, restait à découvrir. Qui se chargerait de la tâche encore
gigantesque? L'exploration française d'avant 1760 avait créé un
type social: le coureur de bois, le traitant, le héros de l'aviron et du
canot. Quelques événements politiques ou militaires ne suppriment
pas d'un coup un type humain. **L'Histoire ignore ces soudaines
ruptures ou disparitions. Dans l'espace libre une force était lâchée;
elle continuerait d'agir, d'autant que l'espace s'offrait toujours
comme un champ indéfiniment extensible**. (Groulx, 1939, p. 7; *my
emphasis*)

The notion that Frenchness (for want of a better word) in North America
has been little more than a regionally-limited survivor — or heritage, as
is often said — of a 17th/18th-century French empire is a remarkably
tenacious one, particularly in the English-speaking world. Both terms, heritage
and survival, necessarily evoke decline, memory and recall of things past,
marginality, even irrationality. Contemporary North American francophone
collectivities can easily be judged from this perspective as struggling against the
great forces of history and civilisation, or the 'natural' course of events that have
led to the identification in the eyes of many professional geographers and of
the public at large of a continent called Anglo-America which extends from the
Mexican border to the Arctic. Accordingly, those who sought in the 1970s, 80s
and 90s to create the new francophone state of Québec on this continent were
widely considered to be leading a struggle more appropriate to the 19th century
and earlier. In the 1970s I heard noted English Canadian scholars voicing such
sentiments and I have often been confronted with puzzled questions from
English people and Australians as to why people speak French in Canada —
and in many quarters, including France, there is utter astonishment that many
Québécois do not speak English at all! To so many citizens of the 'modern

world' it seems inconceivable that a non-hegemonic 'small' society has not long since resigned itself to accommodation and integration into the dominant continental civilisation.

Nothing could be further from the truth than to suggest that Québec and other parts of French America are simply witnesses to a distant past, latter-day relics somehow living on borrowed time. The very term French America is of course of no help in correcting fundamental errors of interpretation, for the continent's francophones are in no sense French. The language may be French, but little else is. Even there, differences in accent and vocabulary between the French spoken in Québec, Acadie or Louisiane, on the one hand, and in metropolitan France, on the other, are considerable. They are of the same order as the distance between English and American, Portuguese and Brazilian, Iberian and Latin American Spanish, and therein lies another problem which is at the source of so many misinterpretations. Four major European languages are spoken in the modern Americas. In the case of English, Spanish and Portuguese, the centre of gravity — with regard to demography, economy, cultural creativity and the production of knowledge — has quite clearly shifted from the Old to the New World in its transition across the Atlantic. Such, however, is not the case with French. The language's centre of power and influence, in both demographic and political terms, is still resolutely European.[1] Québec's voice sits somewhere on the periphery, Acadie's is on a far distant horizon and Louisiane lies far beyond even that. The fact that there is no independent French-speaking state in the Americas — if one excludes the tragic case of Haiti — adds another dimension to the problem of visibility in the international arena.[2]

Yet another problem arises from the fact that, viewed from beyond its shores, North America is seen as tending towards, if not already constituting, a single community of interest. Popular imagination reinforces this view. Mosaics, territories and nations are concepts to be attributed to the past in this view of the continent. So once again Québec is seen to stand alone, whereas Catalonia, Bavaria, Scotland and Wales 'naturally' assert their place in what Denis de Rougemont calls a 'Europe des regions,' (de Rougement, 1977, chapter 12) and Yann Fouéré designates 'L'Europe aux cent drapeaux.' (Fouéré, 1968).

But can the North America above the Rio Grande really be considered a continent devoid of anything but Anglo nations, other than an aberrant

---

1   In practice it extends beyond Europe, but the extension is north-south rather than east-west; across the Mediterranean to the Maghreb and on to West and Central Africa, to produce a political geography sometimes referred to as Françafrique.

2   There again, French is co-official with Creole in Haiti and it is the latter which is the language of everyday life for the vast majority of the population.

Québec? Of course not! Rather, the US and what was for a time called British North America, two imperial powers with resolutely transcontinental aspirations, did everything to efface the ancient nations that stood in their paths and to vigorously counter the birth of any new ones. Consider all the Native American peoples whose names are carefully inscribed on the 17th- and 18th-century maps of the continent: the Esquimaux, the Algonquins, the Hurons, the Illinois, the Sioux, the Nez Percé, the Natchez, the Renards, the Iroquois, the Abenakis, the Cris, the Apaches, the Cherakis and so forth. Their early encounters with the French explain why so many of these bore French names. Then there are those peoples born of contact between the original inhabitants of the continent and the newcomers, notably the Métis Nation, or Bois-Brûlés, a product principally of the merging of French-Canadian (but also Scottish) and Amerindian peoples. The *Métis* had a project to establish a New Nation in Western Canada that would welcome in their midst the oppressed peoples of the world. They had a charismatic leader in Louis Riel, who was hanged for insurrection by the Canadian government in November 1885. They even had a provisional government for a while.

Other peoples with nationalist aspirations included the Mormons, who in the mid 19th century trekked beyond the then boundaries of the US to establish the Kingdom of God on the margins of the Great Salt Lake. In addition, some Black Americans envisioned the creation of an independent state in the American South in the wake of the Civil War. Neither of these endeavours came to fruition, however.

Certainly the one-nation tide has turned in recent decades, notably in Canada, which accorded constitutional recognition to the First Nations and to the *Métis* people in 1983 and sanctioned the creation of the Territory of Nunavut for the Inuit in 1999. But these new collectivities, by virtue of their material dependence, remain essentially wards of the central Canadian state.

From such a perspective Franco-America — for that is what this author insists on calling it (Louder & Waddell, 2008) — appears to stand alone in having survived this hecatomb and, as in the case of modern Québec, has even flourished. But there again this sense of uniqueness is an illusion. An observation by the well-known American anthropologist Renato Rosaldo is particularly revealing. In the course of reviewing a book entitled *Social Change and Psychological Perspectives* for the journal *American Anthropologist*, back in 1973, he casually remarked:

> In the late 1950s at Tucson High School, we Chicanos (for even then
> that is what we called ourselves) sometimes jokingly said we were French
> Canadians. Probably we were thinking about our language and our distant
> but distinctive cultural heritage; or perhaps we had in mind the fact that
> though we had come second, and not first, like the Native Americans, we

had collided equally disastrously with the onrushing manifest destiny of capitalism and the Protestant ethic. (Rosaldo, 1973, p. 1003)

In characterising French Canadians and Chicanos as second-comers, Rosaldo points to the fact that both are products of an earlier imperial age and of an economic order known as mercantilism. Each developed a distinctive identity and, as a corollary, a new name that took form within the political boundaries of the countries now known as Canada and the United States of America. Hence both possess the firm sentiment of being authentic products of continental North America rather than immigrant peoples coming, on the one hand, from beyond the Atlantic and, on the other, from south of the Rio Grande. In the circumstances, it is hardly surprising that some within the Chicano political elite took considerable interest in the Québec independence movement back in the 1970s and 1980.

With regard to names, the term French Canadian only dates back to Confederation, hence to the birth of the modern Canadian state. From 1867 onward, all the country's citizens, the majority of whom had previously been known as English, became Canadians. Prior to that it was only the French-speakers who were referred to as, and who called themselves, *Canadiens* (*Canayens*). This was a clear expression of the fact that a distinctive (with regard to France) identity had taken form on the shores of the St. Lawrence River. The origins of this new nation can be traced back to the very beginning of the colony of New France. The settlers called themselves *habitants* rather than *paysans* and, significantly, they preceded metropolitan France in establishing (Canadian) French as their common language. Many quickly moved out of the confines of the St Lawrence valley to become *coureurs de bois, voyageurs, hivernants*, some merging with Amerindians they encountered in their travels across the continent, thereby giving birth to the *Métis* people.

In this sense, New France was very much a beginning and its demise in 1763, inscribed in the Treaty of Paris, was far from being the end of a collective adventure insofar as the *Canadien* inhabitants of the colony were concerned. Certainly Great Britain succeeded in destroying once and for all a nascent French state in North America, but it failed to efface or crush the ardour of an emergent North American people that was a direct product of New France. Their tradition of movement, which carried with it a strong sense of identity as a people, was established from first settlement, gained increasing momentum after the Conquest, and was sustained throughout the 19th century and well into the next one. Notwithstanding the dominant discourse of the Catholic Church in this time, this geographical expansion was not about 'survival' (*survivance*), but about development and growth, always in a non-hegemonic sense.

Two anecdotes, one personal and the other literary, serve to illustrate this point from a geographical perspective. In the mid 1990s, in my capacity as geography professor at Université Laval, I had an office in the Petit Seminaire de Québec, a magnificent building located in the heart of the walled city and dating back to 1678. The private chapel of the first Bishop of Québec after the Conquest, Mgr Briand (1766–1773), was adjacent to my office. The bishop's jurisdiction covered all of France's former possessions in North America — this, regardless of the changes in political regime. In practice, he focused his attention on American territory in the region of the Great Lakes and the Pays des Illinois. In other words, his vision and his sphere of action extended far beyond what had now been reduced to the Province of Lower Canada.

So much for the reality of continental reach from a Québec base immediately after the Conquest! Some 77 years after British acquisition of Québec, Charles Dickens visited the city, arriving by boat from Montréal. Perched on Cap Diamant and overlooking the St Lawrence River, he was deeply impressed by what he saw and called it 'this Gibraltar of America.'[3] In other words he spontaneously recognised the city to be the key to the continent. In so doing, he gave sense to the idea of the *Canadiens* being a people of America who, from their St Lawrence hearth, journeyed throughout the continent. Their language, too, was a language of America, the language of the fur trade, a language spoken in a thousand communities and institutions across the continent well into the 20th century. And it was a language which, as it spread across the continent, gave birth to new languages, notably Mitchif on the Prairies and Chinook on the Pacific façade of the Rocky Mountains. The terms the early explorers and settlers initially attributed to the St Lawrence River, 'La Grande Rivière de Canada' and 'Le chemin qui marche,' clearly evoke this sense of movement to and from the interior of the continent.

The fact of being *born of America* as distinct from being *immigrants to America*, in terms of self-identification, accounts for the distinctive linguistic and cultural behaviour of Francos — for what other collective name can we give to a people, so heterogeneous and so scattered across the continent — through time and place. They have never felt themselves obliged to change their language or culture as a trade-off for the right to live in any part of the continent. This simple fact of self-perception accounts for the omnipresence of such fundamental expressions of distinctive identity. Admittedly that omnipresence is geographically fragmented, if not indeed highly balkanised, but this enduring characteristic is a mark of its expanse rather than limits. The novelist Clark Blaise illustrates this point well:

3   'The impression made upon the visitor by this Gibraltar of America: its giddy heights; its
     citadel suspended, as it were, in the air; its picturesque steep streets and frowning gateways;
     and the splendid views which burst upon the eye at every turn: is at once unique and
     lasting.' (Dickens, 1842, p. 201).

> My father told it to me one day over beers in a bar in Manchester [New
> Hampshire] as though he were giving me an inheritance. One of my
> uncles, the one who'd gone to California, had taken the easy northern
> route across Ontario and the prairies, then down the west coast lumber
> trails, without missing a single French messe along the way. All America is
> riddled like Swiss cheese, with pockets of French. (Blaise, 1974, p. 159)

The remark was, by the author's own admission, a pure creation of the literary
mind, but it is in fact grounded in reality of human experience, as can be
proven time and again. As the historian Stewart Doty, long-time professor at
the University of Maine and an authority on the Franco-Americans of New
England, stated in the 1980s:

> The first time I heard French spoken in North America, except in a
> classroom, occurred thirty-five years ago in Clifton, Kansas. The speaker
> was my Franco-American landlady, in conversation with her teenage
> daughter. Only in the 1980s … did I finally learn that in the 1860s my
> landlady's people had come on the Rock Island Railroad from Kankakee,
> Illinois. On the banks of the Republican River in Clay and Cloud counties
> they established the only enclave of Francophones in Kansas. Almost one
> hundred years later, at least two of their descendants were able to speak
> French with one another. (Doty, 1989, p. 137)

The Francos of Kansas were, of course, descendants in turn of people who had
settled on the banks of the St Lawrence in the 17th and 18th centuries, later
moved to the Kankakee-Bourbonnais region of Illinois and then followed the
American agricultural frontier to their present destination.

Such anecdotes abound. I came across another one recently in a manuscript
on the Washington Territory (Pacific Northwest). The author, Robert
Foxcurran, in writing about what he calls 'the founding families' of the region,
states:

> Regardless of many of the patronyms of these families having originated in
> the British Isles, the common language of the mixed-blood communities
> was in fact French. Initially, their language was more widely spoken in
> the Pacific Northwest than English. These families and their communities
> continued to speak French well into the 20th century, but it was almost
> extinct by World War II. In this region of the country, French is not
> a foreign language. A closer look at the map or into Chinook Jargon
> makes that clear. Traveling down the Columbia-Snake river system and
> its numerous tributaries, lakes and neighboring topographic features will
> bear this out: the Boise, Portneuf, Payette, Malheur, Grande Ronde, Pend
> Oreille, Coeur d'Alene, Grand Coulee, Dalles, Deschutes, Cascades, and
> Bois(t)fort. (Foxcurran, 2008, p. 4)

French was not only the home language; it was also the spoken (but not the written) language of the fur trade. Officers of the Hudson Bay Company and the Northwest Company had to master it to speak with their men. Americans who ventured into the West, drawn by the trade, had to learn it. For their epic journey of western exploration in 1804–5, Meriwether Lewis and William Clark had to have *Canadiens* and *Métis* as guides, interpreters and entertainers in order to cross the continent and of course they met 'mountain men' on their way, that is other Francos who had journeyed west long before them. With the collapse of the fur trade and the end of continental exploration in the first half of the 19th century, these people and their language were progressively discarded as lacking utility. However, some adjustment was possible, at least provisionally. Many *Métis* took to running the wagon trains that moved through the West, while plurilingual *Canadiens* became interpreters for the US government and its various agencies in their move to marginalise and crush the Native American nations that stood in the way of westward expansion.

Other frontiers — forest, mining, agriculture, industry — swiftly succeeded that defined by fur. *Canadiens*, now being progressively transformed into *Canadiens français*, soon explored them, bringing once again their language and religion, their values and dreams. So Lafontaine (Ontario), St Boniface (Manitoba), Willowbunch (Saskatchewan), Maillardville (British Columbia), Bourbonnais (Illinois), Gentilly (Minnesota), Saint Joseph (Kansas), together with the Little Canadas of Lewiston (Maine), Manchester (New Hampshire), Lowell (Massachusetts) and Woonsocket (Rhode Island) took form, together with hundreds of other *paroisses nationales* scattered across the continent. And here I speak only of migration out of the St Lawrence valley, similar expansionary movements having occurred out of the two other Franco hearth regions of Acadia and Louisiana.

National parishes; *le terme est lâché*! How can this movement, this Franco-American personality, be conceptualised, given what I have said earlier? The Québécois sociologist Fernand Dumont comes closest to answering this question (Dumont, 1997). In migrating across the continent and in settling with fellow-countrymen and kin, the Francos' intention was to *faire société*, that is reproduce the communities of the St Lawrence valley (of Acadie and perhaps Louisiane), with as high a degree of institutional completeness as possible. So classical colleges were created in the US, where *Canadien* history was completely taught in French. Churches, hospitals and orphanages, newspapers, sporting and mutual aid societies were an integral part of the institutional mosaic, the range of institutions and services being determined by the size, wealth and stability of the community. It was, however, a mission ultimately doomed to failure, notably in the US, although typically it took several generations to erode the institutional and linguistic foundations of Franco-America, given the will of the migrants, the solidity of the institutional arrangements provided by the Catholic Church and the strength of external ties, especially with the Québec 'hearth.' Québec in fact only gave up trying to establish communities across the continent in 1953, the last departure comprising a dozen families from Lac St Jean, who moved to northern Alberta with their priest to create the village of St Isidore.

This sense of an identity of continental dimensions finally dissolved in the early 1960s. This development had, of course, been long in coming, thanks to a succession of blows. The main ones were: the formation of the Confederation in 1867; the Great Depression of 1929 and the closure of the US-Canadian border to migration in its wake; the effective institutional collapse of the Catholic Church within French Canada in the early 1960s; and the 1967 meeting of the *États généraux du Canada français*, where the Québec delegation made clear its lack of shared political identity with delegations from the rest of Canada.

Whole pieces of Québec also disappeared with the hanging of Louis Riel in Regina in 1885, the elimination of French from the Legislature of Manitoba in 1890, the closure of the *collège classique* at Bourbonnais (Illinois) in 1938 and the Sentinelliste crisis in New England in 1924–9, not to mention the final assault of the US cavalry at Wounded Knee in 1890:

> Des choses aussi terre à terre que la traite des fourrures et la nécessité
> de survivre nous auront permis, sans même que nous en apercevions,
> de devancer l'Occident entier dans l'aventure sans fin des relations
> interculturelles. Le Français Gilles Havard (*Empires et métissages*, Sillery,
> 2003) oserait-il imaginer qu'en 1890, lorsque la cavalerie américaine
> massacrait le dernier carré de la résistance amérindienne à Wounded Knee,
> c'était un morceau du Québec qui disparaissait? (Lapierre, 2003)

In saying this I am talking as much about a referential world, an *imaginaire* of continental dimensions, as about an elemental geography.

With the birth of contemporary Québec nationalism a tension that had always existed between the *habitant* and the *voyageur* was transformed into a deep wound. From that point on it had become evident that the project to *faire société* could only be realised within the framework of the modern state and would involve a strategic withdrawal into the only place on the continent where francophones constituted the vast majority of the population and could thus proceed with their dream within the framework of democratic institutions. I say 'only', but of course the Acadie of New Brunswick also had good demographic reason to share the same desire, the birth of the Parti Québécois being mirrored by the creation of a Parti Acadien.

What had been an imprecise and eminently fluid boundary between a variety of 'ways of being' was now transformed into a line on the map of the continent, a political boundary, divergent interests and — above all — a fracture of immeasurable depth with the Province of (soon to become l'État du) Québec on one side and the diasporic minority communities of French America on the other.

Quite clearly the Québec project has been a successful one. Although no fully independent francophone state has been created in North America, a vibrant modern nation has emerged, immigrants are more or less successfully integrated into the language and culture of the host society and they contribute to its constant reformulation and renewal. At the same time, a broad variety of Québec corporations successfully engage in continental and global economies. However, this new entrepreneurial face has caused a 'sea-change' in the relationship between the St Lawrence hearth and the rest of the continent and comes at a definite cultural cost.

As Marc Boucher recounts in a recent article on the contemporary Québécois presence in California (Boucher, 2008, pp. 147–66), highly-qualified individuals and businesses in the realms of cinema, medicine, science and technology are drawn to the Golden State. However, their presence is typically of limited duration, interaction with other Francos is largely of an informal nature and close contact is maintained with Québec, where many return as their children grow older. In other words, the high degree of individualism threatens identity, while demographic fluidity — or constant replacement of the population — is the chosen response to this situation of relative cultural and linguistic vulnerability and isolation.

Herein lurks the dilemma of contemporary Québec society. The birth in the 1960s of a new identity that is territorially limited results in the relationship to, and the historical experience of, the larger continent being effaced from collective memory. All that lies beyond the boundaries of the modern state of Québec is effectively transformed into unknown if not indeed resolutely alien territory. Individuals continue to be attracted to the continent beyond and they engage in the dream of new lands and new opportunities, but no collective or institutional arrangements are now provided to support this dream. Hitherto, the Church and popular culture gave sense and meaning to this Continent Québec, but for several decades now neither have had the strength to nourish it. As Thériault points out, a new generation of Québec intellectuals has also played an active role in the effacing of the larger Franco-America:

> L'américanité comme mouvement intellectuel québécois doit se
> comprendre comme un effort visant à inscrire le Québec et son histoire
> dans une logique continentale, principalement étatsunienne. Mais, au
> contraire de la Franco-Amérique qui relie cette histoire à la matrice
> historique du Canada français et à l'existence d'une mémoire francophone,
> l'américanité se veut une manière de rompre avec l'univers canadien-
> français en inscrivant la société québécoise au cœur même du projet

américain, c'est-à-dire en définissant celle-ci comme un type de société possédant des caractéristiques des sociétés neuves, des sociétés du Nouveau Monde, des sociétés de l'Amérique. (Thériault, 2008, p. 356)

Québec's absence of *filiation* with the rest of the continent results in what I can best describe as a referential dissonance, hence a sense of cultural and linguistic ambivalence that can only be attributed tangentially to politics and ideology. Contemporary Québécois identity can, from this geo-historical perspective, be conceived as a contrived one. While in some sense 'new,' the roots of this identity are in reality grounded in the historic duality that associated rootedness with mobility. There were *habitants* on the one hand and *coureurs de bois* on the other, hence Frenchness 'here' and *métissage* 'there', the two geographically and economically linked, with both dating back to the very foundations of New France. The current fracture, and hence denial 'of the world beyond the St. Lawrence valley', has created truncated identities and it is this new reality that lies at the heart of the misrepresentation Francos themselves have of the Franco-American experience.

There is an ironic twist to this tragedy in the sense that many US novelists and scholars incorporate Frenchness into their relating of the American experience. One need only mention, in this regard, the figure of Pasquinel in *Centennial*, James Michener's literary contribution to the bi-centenary of US independence:

> He was a coureur de bois, one who runs in the woods, and where he came from no one knew.
>
> He was a small dark Frenchman who wore the red knitted cap of Quebec, and his name was Pasquinel.
>
> He was a solitary trader with Indians, none better, and in his spacious canoe he carried beads from Paris, silver from Germany, blankets from Canada and bright cloth from New Orleans …
>
> He dressed like an Indian …
>
> As to where he came from, some claimed Montreal and the Mandan villages. Others said they had seen him in New Orleans in 1789. (Michener, 1974, pp. 211, 213)·

In other words *Canadiens* and, of course, *Acadiens* (with Evangéline) figure in some of the founding myths of the US nation. At the same time, this Franco presence is never an enduring reality. Rather, to quote Michel Lapierre, 'Nous hantons la conscience américaine tout en étant l'antithèse vivante de sa nature et de son évolution' (Lapierre, 2001, p. 39). Franco heroes are confined to the 17th and 18th centuries, the present being unequivocally (Anglo-) American.

In Québec the opposite is the case. In creating the modern state it is the continental past which has been effaced or, at least, deprived of sense and purpose, in spite of the continuing presence of Franco communities throughout North America. A quarter-century ago this led political scientist Daniel Latouche to condemn the larger Franco-American realm to silence, to 'the silence of funeral parlours,' a conclusion he drew in his *Le Devoir* review of our first collection addressing the topic, *Du continent perdu à l'archipel retrouvé: Le Québec et l'Amérique française* (Latouche, 1983):

> On peut certes se visiter, s'échanger, se parler et même se confronter, mais dans quel but? C'est comme si on se réunissait la famille, pour simplement se prouver qu'elle existe. Une fois que chacun a fini de retracer la généalogie de ses voisins — Ah! vous êtes le neveu de ma tante Gertrude — le silence s'installe. C'est le silence des salons funéraires.
>
> Quel beau titre que celui de ce livre: *Du continent perdu à l'archipel retrouvé*. Mais un archipel pour quoi faire? En tracer la carte et y dresser des croix? On aurait bien aimé une conclusion à cet itinéraire, mais je suppose que cela est une autre question.

It was the literary giants of Franco-America who were most inspired to weave the many regional and over-arching continental experiences into one great story, thereby drawing the two worlds back together. Jack Kerouac and Gabrielle Roy both dreamed of doing so, for example. But 'devant l'immensité de l'œuvre à écrire' (Lapierre, 2001, p. 43), the task proved too great for them. How, realistically, can one describe a balkanised experience which is essentially vested in the fluid web of family and kin ties and which pays little regard to the institutions of the Church and of the State, or to political boundaries? How can one realistically weave the rooted society of Québec, the Petits Canadas of New England industrial towns, the Cajuns of Louisiana, the rural parishes of the Canadian Prairies and the *Métis* fringes into a single fabric?

Believe it or not this was precisely what Jack Kerouac projected in his initial plans for *On the Road*, the book that established his reputation as a great American writer (Kerouac, 1957):

> All Jack's life, he believed, subconscious thoughts in the French language kept taking him back to 'childhood revelations of the world.' Now at last he was able to begin erecting a novelistic form in which to interpret this process. The new hero he conceived was a French-Canadian well versed in the English language and culture. The hero's companion would be a 'pure' French-Canadian, whom the hero calls 'Cousin,' which among the country folk in Quebec literally means 'my kind.' The two would travel together like Don Quixote and Sancho Panza, and the cousin would continually reprimand the hero for his 'English silliness.' Jack wanted to portray the conflict between the unrelieved gravity of the true, clannish Canuck and

the romantic hopefulness of a Canuck like himself who had set out to conquer the Anglo-American world. (Nicosia, 1983, p. 325)

Of course, in the book that finally emerged, the two characters were transformed into Dean Moriarty (Neal) and Sal Paradise (Jack),[4] the latter evoking 'sale paradis' in French, or Lousy Paradise!

Deep down Kerouac perhaps knew that the task was an impossible one. The gaping fracture between Québec and the rest of Franco-America steeped the Francos themselves in melancholy and a tragic sense of powerlessness. It was for these reasons, perhaps, that Kerouac, in *Visions of Gerard* (Kerouac, 1963), elevated his brother to the status of a saint because he died at the age of nine without knowing America or the English language! Interestingly, too, an entire cycle of Kerouac's novels is devoted to the Duluoz family, a name he fabricated to link Rivière-du-Loup (Dulu), the place of his ancestors on the Lower St Lawrence, and Wizard of Oz (oz), that great American story whose central message is 'You can't go home again'.

Jack Kerouac was, of course, The Great Rememberer. Even his 'road novels', with all their raw energy, are nourished by a certain memory and experience of the continent. The literary critic Michel Lapierre points out:

> Dans les livres de Kerouac, les mots québécois, semés ici et là dans le texte anglais, déconcertent le lecteur américain, mais prouvent hors de tout doute que la connaissance la plus contemporaine du Nouveau Monde reste incomplète sans la maîtrise de la langue québécoise populaire. (Lapierre, 2001, p. 43)

It is just possible that this 'rêve d'une grande littérature sauvage'[5] — the great (Franco-) American novel — is now in the process of being realised. Three recently published books testify to this longstanding desire. The first, by Deni Yvan Béchard, is entitled *Vandal Love* (Béchard, 2006) and relates the post-war continental adventure of a French-Canadian family, whose roots lie in the poor mixed agricultural and fishing villages of the Gaspé Peninsula. It is a genetically cursed family that gives birth to a mix of giants and runts. It is also a family cursed by a cruel mixture of geography and history that projects (or ejects) so many of its members into the far continent to drift without a soul, without bearings. The book evokes, according to one reviewer, '… the eternal theme of

---

4   The one vaguely Irish and the other vaguely Italian, both being ethnic identities that are more familiar and acceptable to post-war Anglo-America.

5   Lapierre begins his article with the statement, in large characters, 'Le rêve d'une littérature du Nouveau Monde, c'est-à-dire le rêve d'une grande littérature sauvage qui, par-delà de la généalogie, remet en cause la vision occidentale en se fondant sur une osmose des univers européen et amérindien, peut seul nous faire saisir la profondeur de notre imaginaire et, du même coup, le caractère unique de l'histoire du Québec' (Lapierre, 2001, p. 39).

the outsider, the outcast, the freak, in the search to find a place, albeit more of the soul than of the corporeal, that can be called home.'[6] The second, Victor-Lévy Beaulieu's magnum opus, *La Grande Tribu* (Beaulieu, 2008), 35 years in the writing, is what the author himself calls a 'grotesquerie' over 900 pages long. It, too, is marked by an incomprehensible duality, this time encapsulated within a single body. The ancestors of Habaquq Cauchon, before coming to Québec, were half men and half pigs. It was this grotesqueness which made them into outlaws, rebels, insubordinates. And it is this 'grotesque', rebellious part of the first inhabitants that has, perhaps, been reduced to submission and silence, and which so desperately needs to be revived and celebrated.

Victor-Lévy Beaulieu has, of course, been one of the giants of the Québec literary scene for over 40 years, producing 70 books to date. Much of his writing is marked by a continental reach that is at the same time firmly grounded in a triumphant — in the sense of being liberated — Québec. It was in a sense inevitable that VLB, an ardent nationalist, would end up writing a book with the scope of *La Grande Tribu*. After all, isn't James Joyce one of his heroes?

In contrast, Deni Yvan Béchard burst on the literary scene 'from nowhere' or, to be more precise, from the distant margins of Franco-America and from another generation. Aged 33 when *Vandal Love* was first published, he was born in Vancouver of a Gaspesian father, a bank robber, and a hippie American mother. His father's marginality, fate and poverty meant that he moved often, his travels taking in New Mexico, Louisiana, Vermont, New York, Toronto, Montréal, Toronto and Rimouski. As Béchard told one critic, 'For a long time I moved every six months' (quoted in Malavoy-Racine, 2008). Not surprisingly, he affirms that it took him 33 years(!) to relate the tragic quest of the descendants of Hervé Hervé, one half of them brutes (the giants) and the other half spiritual beings, even mystics (the runts); a dysfunctional family, each member seeking in their own way to realise their dream … or to escape a tragic destiny. It is a story that evokes an entire people, uprooted and projected into the immensity of America, most of the time experiencing only incomprehension, pain and suffering.

Victor-Lévy Beaulieu and Déni Yvan Béchard were born at opposite ends of Canada, but each is the bearer of a saga grounded in the Gaspé Peninsula. The task that these two writers have set themselves is immense, perhaps unattainable, the one embracing some of the great liberators of the 19th century and the other an entire continent. But they have no choice, for the destiny of the Francos of North America, in all their diversity, is at stake. The inhabitants of Québec and of the entire continent beyond the confines of the St Lawrence Valley experience feelings of incompleteness and insufficiency because they

---

6   This quote, from *Quill and Quire*, is one of several that prefaces the paperback edition of the book (Béchard, 2007).

lack a clear identity which embraces all their geography — both the Québec hearth and the American destiny. One nourished by the diasporal story which inhabits it and one which proposes not a political realm but an *espace pensable*, an *imaginaire*. Kerouac knew that, for he was 'the great rememberer', and it was precisely that which killed him in the end. He knew too much! He understood! Beaulieu knows it; Béchard too, no doubt. Some of Jack's dreams, recounted in his *Book of Dreams* (Kerouac, 1961), are a revelation in this respect. Consider his 'Happy Dream of Canada':

> … the illuminated Northern Land — I'm there at first on Ste. Catherine or some other Boulevard with a bunch of brother French-Canadians and among old relatives and at one point Nat King Cole is there talking with my mother (is not dark, but light, friendly, I call him 'Nat') — We all go to the Harsh Northern School and are sitting (like the gray wood room of Mechanical Drawing class in Bartlett J H shack) and the teacher is a freckled redhaired Scotchman and acts a little contemptuous of the Frenchies, has his favourite teacher's boy in the front row and he too is a sarcastic freckled redhaired British Canadian — I've been close and talkative and like Saintly Ti Jean with everyone so now contemplatively I lean forward and study the situation, watch the teacher and his asskissing sarcastic prototype, and softly, in French, nodding, for I see it all and only because an outsider American Genius Canuck can see, 'Ca-na-da' — (I say) Ca-na-daw — and my brother darkhaired anxious angry Canucks vehemently agree with me — 'It's always them!' they cry and I see that sarcastic non-French smirk on the redheaded faces, something hateful I must have seen on Ste. Catherine St. in 1953 March, that arrogant Britishfied look — or from ancestors' memories of old French-Indian canoe wars — Had I gone back to Canada I wouldn't have taken shit one from any non Frenchman of Canada … took everything from Brother Noel and mourned — but God the fist smashed face of my redhaired English Canadian enemy —
>
> This was such a happy dream, I woke up at 5 AM from the comradeship and glow of it — no anger (as now, afternoon) at all — I should have written it at dawn — **it was Ti Jean the happy Saint back among his loyal brothers at last** — That's why. (Kerouac, 1961, pp. 117–8; *my emphasis*)

This represents a dream of returning home, to Montréal, to a place where one belongs. It means no more searching, no more solitude, because the quest for home is over. Is this the message that is emerging from Michel Tremblay's trilogy, two of which, *La Traversée du continent* and *La Traversée de la ville*, have recently been published, while the third, *La Traversée des sentiments*, is in the making? Who could be more urban, more Québécois, more Montréalais than Michel Tremblay? And yet in *La Traversée du continent* he discloses that his mother, Rhéauna, was born in Providence (Rhode Island), the daughter of Maria Desrosiers who, as an adolescent in search of liberty, had fled the solitude and oppression of Sainte-Maria-de-Saskatchewan, a tiny French-Canadian community in the prairies. There, she went to work in a textile mill, met a Frenchman and had three girls by him, Rhéauna, Béa and Alice.When Rhéauna was five he died at sea and because her mother was unable to cope, she sent the children back to Saskatchewan to be raised by their grandparents in a 'maison au milieu de nulle part'. Some five years later, the message arrives that Maria, now living in Montréal, wants her eldest daughter to join her. It is this journey back to her mother which is young Rhéauna's 'traversée du continent'; three days on a train with stopovers at night in Regina, Winnipeg and Ottawa, in each of which she is welcomed by relatives. On the last night, between Ottawa and Montréal, Nana (Rhéauna) dreams that the 'house in the middle of nowhere' is in flames and that her grandmother rushes inside to save someone ... someone who does not exist:

> 'Grand-maman! Grand-maman! Y a personne! Y a personne, grand-maman, ça sert à rien de chercher, y a personne!'
>
> La maison s'écroule dans un craquement sinistre.
>
> C'est fini, ils sont morts tous les deux, grand-maman Joséphine et la personne qui n'existe pas.
>
> Elle ouvre la bouche, elle crie, elle pleure. Elle est figée dans une grimace d'horreur et hurle en silence dans la nuit qui crépite.
>
> Grand-papa pose une main sur son épaule.
>
> **'C'est pour ça que tu t'en vas à Montréal, Nana. Pour que la lignée des Desrosiers continue.'** (Tremblay, 2007, p. 279; *my emphasis*)

The Desrosiers, 'cette famille d'errants disséminés à travers le continent, avec leur existence discrète faite d'humbles gestes répétés à l'infini' (Tremblay, 2007, p. 247), the Cree Indian blood that flows in their veins, the distant ancestor who fought at Louis Riel's side and was hung alongside him at Regina, the continual search for a place to settle down and to live in peace; it's all there.

We have yet to see the third and final volume in Michel Tremblay's trilogy, but in this first one Rhéauna is condemned, at the age of ten, to cross the continent in order to be reunited with her mother. In so doing she abandons the solitude of a small French-Canadian community established (provisionally?) in the prairies for the relative comfort of Montréal: 'En Saskatchewan c'est difficile, c'est une lutte de tous les jours; au Québec, c'est du moins ce qu'on dit, c'est plus facile parce qu'il y a plus de gens qui parlent français' (Tremblay,

2007, p. 32). In exploring this theme, the search for home, the path of Michel Tremblay, writing in Key West (Florida), crosses that of Victor-Lévy Beaulieu, in Trois-Pistoles (Québec) and that of Deni Yvan Béchard, whose literary journey starts in the mountains of British Columbia. Collectively, they provide all the ingredients of a cruel tension inscribed in individual families and in an entire people where, on the one hand, the St Lawrence lowlands evoke comfort and security but also naivety and resignation while, on the other, the vast American continent beckons offering hope but also endless wandering, solitude and deception.

This tension illustrates the extent to which geography holds the key to the memories of Québec and of all Franco-America. It is a particular geography that embraces both *heritage* and *destiny*, the former being *Canadien* and the latter unequivocally American, generous in its geography and openness to other peoples and experiences, but ultimately cruel and uncompromising in the conditions it imposes. It is a continuously unfolding drama which explains the necessary grounding of a people in Québec and their need to traverse the continent in all directions. As Michel Tremblay is now slowly revealing, even the roots of Plateau Mont Royal extend like rhizomes far beyond the horizon. The story goes that as a small child: 'le petit Michel grimpait avec amour sur elle et se refugiait sur ses "deux oreillers", c'était son bateau, son port, son capitaine, c'était sa mer et avant de s'endormir il lui disait: "Katchewan!"' (Lévesque, 1994).

REFERENCES

Beaulieu, Victor-Lévy (2008) *La Grande Tribu. C'est la faute à Papineau. Grotesquerie* (Trois-Pistoles: Éditions Trois-Pistoles).

Béchard, Deni Yvan (2006) *Vandal love: a novel* (Toronto: Doubleday Canada); paperback edition (Anchor Canada, 2007).

Blaise, Clark (1974) *Tribal Justice* (Garden City: Doubleday and Co).

Boucher, Marc (2008) 'Les Québécois au pays des "rêves": nouveaux enjeux, nouvelles tendances en Californie', in Dean Louder and Eric Waddell (eds.), *Franco-Amérique* (Québec: Septentrion), pp. 147–66.

Brouillette, Benoît (1939) *La pénétration du Continent américain par les Canadiens français* (Montréal: Granger Frères).

de Rougemont, Denis (1977) *L'avenir est notre affaire* (Paris: Stock).

Dickens, Charles (1842) *American Notes for General Circulation*, Vol. II (London: Chapman and Hall).

Doty, C. Stewart (1989) 'Commentary', in Stephen J. Hornsby, Victor A. Konrad and James J. Herlan (eds.) *The Northeastern Borderlands: Four Centuries of Interaction* (Fredericton: Acadiensis Press), pp. 137–9.

Dumont, Fernand (1997)'Essor et déclin du Canada français', *Recherches sociographiques*, 38 (3), pp. 419–67.

Fouéré, Yann (1968) *L'Europe aux cent drapeaux: essai pour servir à la construction de l'Europe* (Paris: Presses d'Europe).

Foxcurran, R. R. (2008) *Washington Territory (WT)'s Tale of Two Frenchtowns*, unpublished manuscript.

Groulx, Lionel, M. l'Abbé (1939) *Préface*, in Benoît Brouillette, *La pénétration du Continent américain par les Canadiens français* (Montréal: Granger Frères), pp. 7–8.

Havard, Gilles (2003) *Empires et métissages* (Sillery, Quebec: Septentrion).

Kerouac, Jack (1957) *On the Road* (New York: Viking Press).

Kerouac, Jack (1961) *Book of Dreams* (San Francisco: City Lights Books).

Kerouac, Jack (1963) *Visions of Gerard* (New York: Farrar, Straus and Company).

Lapierre, Michel (2001) 'Le rêve de la grande littérature sauvage', *La revue de l'Aut'Journal*, 1 (1), pp. 39–43.

Lapierre, Michel (2003) 'Métis de souche et métis de cœur', *Le Devoir* (3 May).

Latouche, Daniel (1983) 'Du continent perdu à l'archipel retrouvé,' *Le Devoir* (10 August).

Lévesque, Robert (1994) Review of *Un ange cornu avec des ailes de tôle* (Michel Tremblay, Montréal: Leméac/Actes Sud), *Le Devoir* (11–12 June).

Louder, Dean and Eric Waddell (eds.) (1983) *Du continent perdu à l'archipel retrouvé: Le Québec et l'Amérique française* (Ste-Foy: Les Presses de l'Université Laval; new edn. 2007).

Louder, Dean and Eric Waddell (eds.) (2008) *Franco-Amérique* (Québec: Septentrion).

Malavoy-Racine, Tristan (2008) 'D.Y. Béchard: La dérive du continent', *Voir* (17 January).

Michener, James A. (1974) *Centennial* (Greenwich: Fawcett Crest).

Nicosia, Gerald (1983) *Memory Babe: A Critical Biography of Jack Kerouac* (New York: Grove Press).

Rosaldo, Renato (1973) Review of *Social Change and Psychological Perspectives* in *American Anthropologist*, 75: 1003.

Thériault, Joseph Yvon (2008) 'À quoi sert la Franco-Amérique?' in Dean Louder and Eric Waddell (eds.), *Franco-Amérique* (Québec: Septentrion), pp. 355–65.

Tremblay, Michel (2007) *La Traversée du continent* (Montréal: Leméac).

Tremblay, Michel (2008) *La Traversée de la ville* (Montréal: Leméac).

2

THE HEAD OF THIS RIVER IS UNKNOWN! ... BETWEEN *TRUCHEMENT* AND *METISSAGE*: THE *CANADIEN'S TRAJECTOIRE* IN THE FORMATION OF THE AMERICAS

Jean Morisset

It is enlightening and amusing to note the geographic names supplied
by the voyageurs. To be sure, they merely translated many of them
from the Indian names, but who among the white men knew enough
of the native's speeches to translate them? Few traders could deal with
the Indians except through an interpreter or truchement, usually a
voyageur [a *Métis*] or a half-breed. (Nute, 1955, p. 259)

English penetration inland will adopt French habits in the service of
English goals. (Franklin, p. 49).

Sacré enfant de Grâce, he would exclaim, mixing English, French,
and Spanish into a punchero-like jumble, voyez-vous dat I vas nevare
tan pauvre as dis time; mais before I vas siempre avec plenty café,
plenty sucre; mais now, God dam, I not go à Santa Fé, God dam, and
mountain man [coureurs de coulées et de montagnes] dey come aquí
from autre côté, drink all my café. Sacré enfant de Grâce, nevare I vas
tan pauvre as tis time, God dam. I not care comer meat, ni frijole, ni
corn, mais widout café I no live. I hunt may be two, three day, may be
one week, I eat nothin; mais sin café, enfant de Grâce, I no live, parce
que me not sacré Espagnol, mais one [oune] french-man.
Spoken by a mountain man named Laforey [Laforest?], collected by
the British traveller George Frederick Ruxton and extracted from
Adventures in Mexico and the Rocky Mountains (1847). Quoted in
Blevins (1993), p. xi and p. 226.

C'était un canot indien [près de Saginaw et] l'homme qui était
accroupi au fond de cette fragile embarcation portait le costume et
avait toute l'apparence d'un Indien […] Comme je me préparais

[…] à y monter, le prétendu Indien s'avança vers moi, me plaça
deux doigte sur l'épaule et me dit avec un accent normand qui me
fit tressaillir: "N'allez pas trop vitement, y en a des fois ici qui s'y
noient". Mon cheval m'aurait adressé la parole que je n'aurais pas, je
crois, été plus surpris. J'envisageai celui qui m'avait parlé et dont la
figure frappée des premiers rayons de la lune reluisait alors comme
une boule de cuivre: "Qui êtes-vous donc, lui dis-je, le français semble
être votre langue et vous avez l'air d'un Indien?" Il me répondit
qu'il était un bois-brûlé, c'est-à-dire le fils d'un Canadien et d'une
Indienne. (Vallée, 1973, p. 57).

You know at this time, there were only the Indians and the French,
the white people came much later.
From the recollections of an old Cree Woman from Saskatchewan.

Québec, *haut-lieu* of the First America …
Québec, soul City of the Americas.

Québec, cradle of French America,
Québec, bosom of a nameless America.

Québec, Gibraltar of the New World
Québec, bastion of British North America.

So many evocative expressions paying tribute to Québec,
So many names attempting to capture its essence.

But where is Québec located within the destiny of the Americas?
Where is Québec spiritually and geographically?

*

History, history … memory of memory. Farther from us than the hidden side of the moon, as Octavio Paz said in one of his poems. Why write novels, poetry and essays when the majority of your population is illiterate? Carlos Fuentes was once asked. To fill the emptiness and seal the immense gaps that our historians have refused to examine, he replied.

Canada … *Amérique canadienne* … *Canadien* America,[1] grounded in cultural *métissage* since the earliest founding of Québec, evolved into a Franco-Creole America that has survived conquests and the rule of empires to sustain its rhythm and unbridled richness hidden beneath the rubble of unspoken histories. It is therefore impossible to understand the *Canadien* quest for

1   The original spellings, *Canadien* and *Canayen*, are adopted here.

identity, the memory of a diversified *Métis* Canadian America, without dodging the claims contemporary Canada has made based upon colonial lies and political usurpation. Such an understanding also necessitates moving beyond the idea of either a French America or a British America to embrace the notion of a Franco-America that extends beyond the national political boundaries of the American continent. A pan-American perspective is essential because *Canadiens* are, by origin and destiny within the Americas, the product of an intermingling with other elements of the Americas that has flowed through our geographical blood from the beginning. But, apart from the wind and the snow, the rivers and the lakes, the forests, the rocks and a few inspirational or enigmatic Northern Lights, who can claim to hold any geographic truth?

At the same time — and therein lies the paradox — it is just as impossible to begin an inquiry into *canadienne* oral history and geographical *trajectoire* without thoroughly examining and challenging French America and British America. Both have interpreted and inscribed *Canadien* America from the standpoint of Europeans and, by extension, the world. They have prescribed, scolded, vilified and occasionally celebrated the *Canayens'* identity, the illiteracy and *mouvance sauvage* upon which we are grounded as a people. Consequently, the elusive nature of *Canadien* America's forefathers and native mothers can only come to light through tales and accounts appropriated by the conquering powers. This has resulted in most of today's *Francos* and Native *Canadiens* only being able to discover their past and present by reverting to English language interpretations of their own usurped identity and storytelling.[2] It is a story no official narratives dare to tell and one the British American narrative (or Canadian, to use the appropriated name) has seldom been willing to relate, not to mention the Québec narrative, which denies its *canayennes* and *métisses* roots.

*

The events commemorating the 400th anniversary of the founding of Québec necessitated celebration of virtually the whole of Native French America, leading one to reflect upon the nature of the *Canadien* adventure in America. And this bears directly upon the identity and destiny of *homo canadensis* in the New World. The knell has sounded long and often for the *Canadien*, while celebrating his greatness at the very moment he reached his zenith, just as happened with the Native Indian, draped in the dignity of his presumed extinction. It is why one cannot speak of 'The 400th' without wondering what it is all about, other than a place located and dated by Europe under the mark of Champlain. A pre-Columbian — or pre-Champlanian — site once existed on the banks of the St Lawrence where Québec now sits. Called Uepishtikueiau in

---

2   An America of some 25 to 30 million people of Franco origin (Louder & Waddell, 1983).

Montagnais (Innu), it has recently been re-documented as a place of exchange, of linkage, upon which the French colonial structure was grafted that would be taken over by England. So much so, that we are left with multiple layers of transversal and inter-calcareous memorial sediment which are impossible to sort out, despite the veil of official interpretations seeking to single out the French influence.

This is why we should ask one question from the start. What founding principles can the people of the *Franco-Métis* world of North America call to mind when the only texts which have expressed their reality are those of their apocryphal memory, drained of the written word — a truncated and composted memory, better serving the ferment of Anglo-imperial America and the Yankee states which fed from them and plundered their remains ...

In his 'Memoire of fire', the Latino writer Eduardo Galeano attempted the impossible: a recreation of the birth of the Americas from the codices which were burned and consumed in Tenochtitlan on the Zócalo of Mexico. In his writings, Miguel-León Portilla constantly referred to the Maya codex and others as the most antiquated books of the Americas. This is the literal source of our birth and of our identity as Americans with respect to what the Europeans called the New World. Thus, the cathedral of Mexico is built upon the ashes of the first word. As for we *Canadiens*, what savage, pre-Cambrian cathedral covers us? How can you not rise to the crest of the horizon, the height of your destiny, and shout 'Canada, Canada! Québec, Québec, who are you, where are you?' Where did the initial path originate which projected you into existence? Where is your geographic awareness deposited and which vaults conceal the latent memory of your origins? Like all the words consumed by fire, do we await just as many consumed by the cold?

Over and above official narratives, the 400th anniversary of Québec afforded an indisputable opportunity to ask the fundamental question which haunts all *Amériquains*.[3] Who are we or what are we? Whether or not we define ourselves as Québécois with respect to the New World, what identity do we have — as *Canadiens* first and foremost — in the eyes of our compatriots in the Americas from Alaska to Patagonia? My objective here is to explore the theme 'between *truchement* and *métissage*', the *Canadien* in the trajectory and imaginary universe of the Americas, and discern the place of the *Canadien* among the heroes and characters who inspired and forged the New World.

The *Canadien voyageur* or *coureur de bois* lives on as one of the grand and nameless heroes in the above-mentioned imaginary universe to the same extent

3   The 18th-century French designation *amériquain* rather than *américain* is used here to refer to the whole hemisphere since the USA has appropriated the latter term as the descriptor for its territory. *Amériquain* also signifies the existence of a Franco-America that lies beneath and across the present-day USA.

as the *bandeiante* (banner bearer) and the *cangaceiro* (honourable bandit) from Brazil and the *nègre-marrons*, the pirates and buccaneers of the Caribbean Basin, not to mention Mexico's revolutionary *bandito* and the legendary *cholo-caboclo* (mixed Amerindian and European ancestry). Within that lineage, we should not forget the *Métis* Louis Riel,[4] a descendant of the *voyageur*, the only remnant to still haunt the conscience of British America. How does he fit in with the likes of Tiradentes, Pontiac, Jefferson, Toussaint l'Ouverture, Simón Bolívar, Kondiaronk, Tupac Amarus, Emiliano Zapata, and John Brown? And we should not dismiss Kateri Tétakouita, la Corriveau, Maria Chapdelaine, Sacajawéa and all the half-forgotten heroines of a *Franco-Amérique* that ignores itself in ignoring them.

*

A quest intertwined with that of the *amériquain* hemisphere underlies the evocation of Québec and the Grande Rivière de Canada (Figure 1), a stream that, under its Christianised name of St Lawrence — along with the Meschacébé-Mississippi — fashioned practically all of North America west of the Appalachians and north of the Rio Grande. It begs a question about the *Canadien* spirit concealed beneath the imagination and exploration of *la Nord-Amérique*. Moreover, it is about the subliminal and occulted existence of the *Canadien*, whose almost ubiquitous presence forestalled the arrival of officially recognised explorers, causing him to be relegated to an inferior position in the celebration of imperial history.

As in Mexico and Brazil, Hispanic and Lusitanian America, the web of so-called *Amérique française* or French America is twofold: a European version of the facts, the dreams and the verbalisation. In contrast though, a *Canadien* version, Native and *Métis*, does exist. What appears clear for *Latino-Amérique* is not applicable to Creole *Franco-Amérique du Nord* which bears the name of Canada. Why? Like Hispano-America and Luso-America, Franco-America is a product of the American hemisphere in its entirety to a much larger extent than Anglo-America. From the boreal forests to the Caribbean, Franco-America is situated south of the USA, crossing Saint-Domingue and the entire arc of the Antilles (Ante-Isles) to Guyana and stretching eventually to Amazonia. However, unlike the other three colonial Americas, native French America has never achieved unification in any way, shape or form.

There are two obvious reasons for this. By seeking to 'britishify' Canada

---

4   Louis Riel particularly embodies the grandeur, destiny and tragedy of *l'homo Canadensis*. His political assassination by hanging, in 1885, represents the propitiatory murder of British America (promulgated in 1867 by the British North America Act) which progressively usurped Canada's very name. For more on Riel, see Braz 2005, pp. 79–88; 2003, p. 245. See also Morisset, 1997.

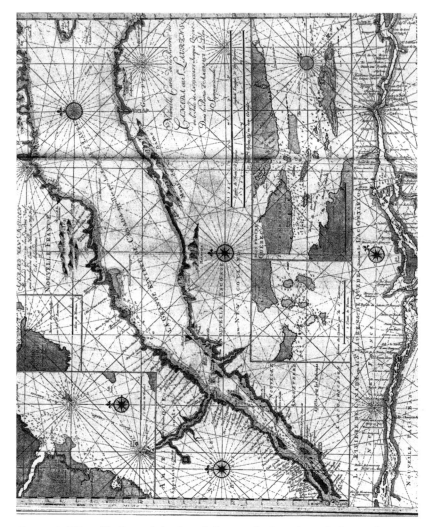

Figure 1: 'Nouvelle Carte de la Grande Rivière de Canada ou St Laurens'.

over two and a half centuries, London and the British Empire have dissociated Canada itself and French Native America from the rest of the Americas and their sister republics emerging in Latin America. Moreover, the prevailing idea of a New France or of a French America serves to systematically conceal its *Canadien* or franco-savage (Indian) roots, into which the Frenchman rapidly disappeared and was unconsciously subsumed by the first America. So much has been asserted about this that one can only wonder by what twist of history the idea of a French America still persists. This is compounded by the fact that

'French America' is less French than Native and as much *Métis* as *Canadien*, both identities tending to merge. There is a consensus forming on this subject.[5]

Hence, there is a *Canadien* America with more resemblance to Brazil and the Caribbean (of which it is, in any case, an extension) than to the Anglo-America of the Atlantic colonies. Colonial France was not really interested in Canada because of her supremacy in the Antilles. Reciprocally, Canada owes its permanence less to France than to the native world without which it would not have existed and could not have survived (Morisset, 1987a, pp. 87–98; 1987b, pp. 32–40; 1996). Paradoxically, however, the idea of a French America excluding the Caribbean being limited strictly to Canada is so deeply ingrained that it is easy to miss the fact that, from an *Ameriquain* perspective, it consists less of a French America than a *Métis* America determined by the interplay of indigenous alliances.

Of the four hegemonic powers — Spain, Portugal, France and England — that intended to divide the New World up between them, only France would be unsuccessful in retaining the vast and geographically fluid expanses it laid claim to. Thus, in contrast to the other Americas, Franco-America still has not achieved unification, except perhaps in an imaginary sense. A further essential dimension that has been obstinately ignored is the fact that French America/*Canadien* America gradually became an in-between America. By that I mean — and I cannot stress this enough — that through the very process of its disappearance, *Canadien* America served to create Anglo-America rather than to recreate itself. However, it remained present, hidden beneath the *bayous mesas, coulées* and *portages* in the subsequent formation of contemporary Native America — with its beadwork, patterns and designs[6] — and, following the movement of refugees from Saint-Domingue to New Orleans after Haitian independence, contributed to the fabrication of Black America, which produced the word 'jazz' from the Creole words *jase* and *jaser* (to speak informally).

*

If a new world emerged from an America that Québec City was to commemorate by celebrating the 400th anniversary of its founding, it is necessarily constituted

5   See, for example, the work of Havard and Vidal, particularly the synthesis, 'Making New France New Again' (2007).

6   Among the numerous texts written by Brasser on this subject, see in particular 1985, p. 225: 'It can be demonstrated that the floral design connection [running throughout Native tribes of Western North America] is with the Roman Catholic missions, beginning on the St. Lawrence River and moving west through the Great Lakes region … the subsequent migration of Red River métis groups into the most remote corners of the greater Northwest, the métis [canadien] art style put its stamp on the art of practically every tribal group of the northern plains and the North West Territories.'

of people born of the *eaux-qui-roulent* (waters which roll) and the *chemin-qui-marche* (way that walks), the original designations of the Grande Rivière de Canada, the St Lawrence. In the 1540s, Jacques Cartier, a navigator from Saint-Malo, identified a new people, bivouacing in snow-laden huts scattered across a seemingly limitless space, as the 'Kingdom of Canada'. Situated high above the edge of the narrowing channel between Hagouchonda and Aquechenunda, a place initially called Stadacona by the Malouins (men of Saint-Malo), it eventually became Québec. But who and what is this remarkable new people which appeared between the parentheses of an evanescent Europe and dawning of a new era and the formation of a new land?

At the centre of a map drawn in London two years after the Royal Proclamation of 1763 (Figure 2), which aimed to determine the destiny of conquered Canada and simultaneously dispose of Native French and *Canadien* America, Major Robert Rogers, the British North America colonial militia leader, inscribed 'the Head of this River is unknown'. Doesn't this phrase speak for itself? Which head, exactly? There is an inscription, 'Missouri', but what is the source of this river? It is unlikely to refer to the head of the *Canadien* or *Canayen*[7], which has always been relatively unknown. In light of this, it is immediately tempting to *partir en dérouine*[8] towards the vast reaches of the Mississippi, that is, the Meschacébé … the Father of Waters, la Grande Rivière Métisse (the Great Métis River), constantly asking ourselves whether the whole of Franco America disappeared from the history of the Americas and continues to elude us. The more one thinks about it, the more it becomes apparent that Native French America, the Canada of the first colonial period, was a basic component of the Americas, which as years passed would be cast from the Americas by its incorporation into British America.

A careful examination of this map is compelling for it reveals a fictional Anglo-America, half Yankee, half British, seeking eagerly and greedily to understand the nature of the gift received from France, via the Peace of Paris, in exchange for Guadeloupe. To all intents and purposes, North America appears here in its entirety, a vast crescent stretching from Labrador or New Britain, with its Eskimeaux [sic] in the north-east, to the Western Sea and the Afsiniboils located on its banks in the south-west. Continuing in an arc, one sees the Mountains of Bright Stone (Rockies) to the south, the Great River Ourigan[9] and New Albion. Then, from south-west to north-east, New Mexico,

---

7   *Canadiens* called themselves *Canayens* just as *Acadiens* were *Cadiens* or *Cayens*.

8   The expression used by the *Métis* of the Prairies to describe departures for great buffalo hunts and lengthy trading missions, from which participants might never return.

9   This mighty river, named by the *voyageurs* and *coureurs de bois*, came, half a century later, to bear the English name of Columbia. The substantive *ourigan* is the *Canadien* pronunciation of *ouragan*, a word borrowed from the Algonquian word for a sack containing chewing

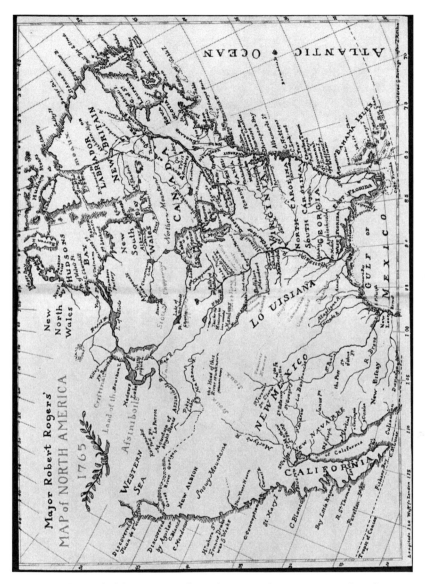

Figure 2: 'The Head of this River is Unknown': Major Robert Rogers' map of North America, 1765.

Louisiana and Virginia. North of the Great Lakes is a Canada considerably reduced in size situated around Hudson's Bay, New South Wales and New

tobacco. Moreover, the word still exists in a tune from *Canayen* folklore: 'ton p'tit ouragan mon ami, ton p'tit ourigan mon gars'.

North Wales. As for the 13 colonies, they stretch from the Atlantic to the Mississippi, although Louisiana remains under Franco-Spanish jurisdiction.

Indeed, there is a striking contrast between the former Continental Canada of the French colonial realm — adjoining Mexico and close to the 'Island of California' (the name coined by French explorers three centuries before), see Figure 3 — and a New England that has expanded to a mind-blowing extent as a result of the conquest of 1759. Canada, in complete contrast to the

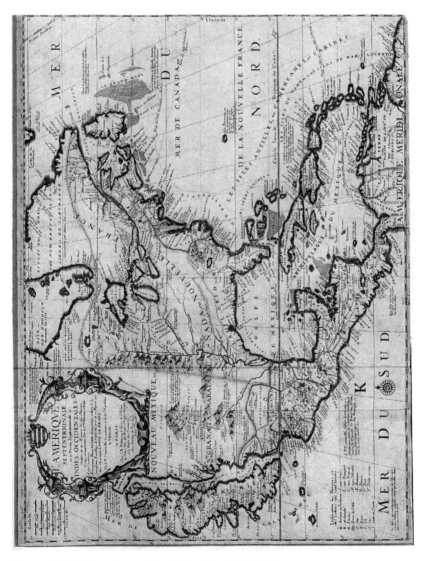

Figure 3: 'L'Amérique Septentrionale' (Province de Québec).

massively-enlarged British colonies, practically disappeared in the new order and was subsumed into a 'territorial reservation' named Province de Québec, specially created by the government in London to enclose all Canadians.[10] This Province is the very entity that serves as the virtual ancestor and model for all Bantustan subject to the Empire. Apart from the Province de Québec and the boundaries between the 13 colonies, practically no other borders exist on this vast continent. A faint dotted line denotes a promontory separating the basins of Louisiana, New Mexico and Florida, but that is all. What a gift! 'For you know,' said Voltaire in 1758, 'that these two nations (France and England) are at war over a few acres of snow in Canada and they are spending for this wondrous war much more than Canada is worth!' To Voltaire therefore, and indeed to the mother country, the *Canayen* was worth little. Perhaps nothing expressed this better than the official reply to the Comte de Bougainville, who bore the Marquis de Montcalm's request for reinforcements and foodstuffs to be sent from France in anticipation of the tumultuous battle for control of North America in 1759, 'When the house is on fire, don't worry about the stables'.

Returning to these stables of continental dimension, two aspects stand out: first, the centre of the map is almost empty, because the 'Head' — the head of America — is unknown. Further, as one moves away from the lands facing the Atlantic, most names of places and Indian nations are in French (Comanches, Sioux, and Cristinaux, for example) or in Spanish (la Barranca, New Navarre). English toponyms only reappear near the shores of the Pacific, from Bay Little Known, located on the west of the peninsula of California, northward to New Year's Haven. Far from being a simple map, this document turns out to be a novel with chapters characterised by their oral nature, begging to be expressed out of an infinite silence drawn from a deep well of memories. Who is the author of the geographic slogan produced by Major Rogers, if not some head of a disguised Native French America in the process of being quickly engulfed by the gestation of Anglo Manifest Destiny?

---

10 This British initiative marked the first extension of the name of Québec from the city
    to a wider area [the whole of Canada becoming Québec]. The probable intent was to
    distinguish the Saint Lawrence heartland, home of the majority of the French population
    in North America, from the vast former French empire on the continent that, apart from
    Louisiana, the British now controlled (Hayes, 2002, p. 114). In fact, this Province of
    Québec constitutes a sort of Bantustan, before it became known as such, establishing all the
    inaccessible *Canadiens* who were too numerous to be deported as the *Acadians* had been.
    The British unsuccessfully sought to compel all *Canadiens* to remain there, but this enclave
    dissolved with the Québec Act (1774) when London extended the territory of Québec all
    the way to the Great Lakes, including the Ohio Valley.

*

It is clear that British America is less a daughter of Albion than an heir to a gloriously intermixed and entwined amalgamation of *Canayens* and *Savages*, which England initially sought to transform into Canada and that contemporary Québec later aimed to change into a French America rather than to recreate a *Franco-Amérique* or an *Amérique créole* and *métisse*.

> To summarise:
> *Amérique française*, French America … Native French America, what does it mean?
> In answering that question one cannot fail to discover the history and evolution of all the Americas from Native Alaska to Patagonia.
> Geographical memory has been appropriated by historical hijacking, which ends up being represented as the sole and true history.
> So it was not Champlain who founded Québec, but rather Québec that founded Champlain.
> And it was Québec, not England, which founded British America.

That is the history of Canada-Québec! The destiny of a forever-fragmented *Canadien* America that has percolated under the Dominion of Canada and a half-forgotten native North America and has continued to exist under the USA's colonial rule, 'God is my right' and 'In God we trust'. It is a reality somewhat difficult to perceive within the physical and spiritual boundaries of contemporary Québec. Not once in their history have the people known as Québécois had the opportunity of participating in the process of establishing the frontiers to which they have become subject. Hence, despite being aware of its *Métis* roots, French Native America has not been able to come to grips with this knowledge. It cannot get rid of the names and interpretations imposed through the accumulation of the successive conquests that have succeeded in marking the land and the collective consciousness, legal constraints having seized control of the North American imagination. What a challenge it is to try and bear witness to it. What a challenge to expose the fallacies of commonly accepted geographic history in order to regain one's rightful place in a hinterland covering three-quarters of the North *Amériquain* hemisphere, knowing full well that once that identity has been reassumed it is likely to be swiftly threatened by extinction.

*

And so — far from being a fortified bastion, tucked behind its garrison and watching the Grande Rivière de Canada go by — Québec forms the foundation of an empire never fully established but never entirely shattered. This empire, based on a first America that has little or nothing to do with today's Canada and US, has never understood who controlled it — Natives or French — but perceives a geographic transfusion between the two leading to the formation of a third person: the *Canadien*. To eliminate any misunderstanding, it must be remembered that after first singling out this term for Natives, the French then gave the name *Canadien* to their own Indianised Creoles born in America and whose identity was moulded by their inter-relationship with the indigenous peoples and physical geography of the so-called New France. Who then are *Canayens* and what has become of them? It is perhaps less important to answer this question than to examine the geographical and historical influences, like an explorer looking for clues along a riverbed which is difficult to follow.

*

At this point, let me tell you a story. Upon my return several years ago from a journey along the meandering Oregon trails which have been depicted in narratives and travel stories, I chanced upon a character whose route I knew, but whose voice I had never heard, whom the Anglos called Mountain Man. This emblematic figure travelled longitudinally for more than a century along the vast complex of ridges, valleys, plateaus and grabens stretching north and south along the Rockies overlooking the Prairies to the coastal chains of the Pacific. For this reason he was placed in a new category, evolving from *coureur de bois* to *coureur de coulées* and *coureur de canyons*. In coming across the words of a man called Laforest in Frederick Ruxton's text cited at the beginning of this chapter, a man whose strangeness and unpredictability would qualify him to be a member of a lost tribe of Israel, I felt I had discovered the missing link in the great chain of our errant identity.

Clearly, Ruxton puts words in his mouth. Laforest would never have said that he was 'oune Frenchman', but rather a *Canayen*, a trader of furs from the tribe of wandering *Canadiens*. At that moment, I became fully conscious of the existence of a land and citizens without bounds, recognised by all and named '*Canadien* America'. In addition, for more than a century this errant Canada adjoined on its southern flank another land without a northern border, namely Mexico. As a result, a language of trade was born of these contacts, a kind of Creole that reflected the interdependence of the *Canayen voyageur*, the Mexican *pocho* and the south-westernised English of the first cowboys venturing forth into these lands. In short, a jargon of shifting vocabulary emerges from the bowels of the errant *Canadien* constantly slipping through the layers of history in search of an undiscoverable place to lay down their troubled soul, which, nevertheless, they would never exchange for any other.[11]

11 I have written various texts on this theme: Morisset 1992a, 1992b, 1994, 1996, 1998, 2001, 2008.

A good story should be backed up by personal experience. In the mid 1960s, while I was working for the fish and game commission at Great Slave Lake, I encountered a game warden named René Mercredi. No, not René Wednesday, but Mercredi — probably transformed phonetically into French from the name McGillvery or similar. In a soft, flowing English, he invited me to visit the cabin where his family was spending the summer. Apart from a quick 'Nice day. Good (*goude*) to meet you', his wife, also *Métis*, had not said a word. Being too busy preparing the meal, she let her beautiful, round and happy face do the talking. When she served me a plate of stew, I tasted a little, looked attentively at my hostess, smiled, then tasted again, telling her in English, 'Hmm! This stew has a French flavour'. I hardly had time to add that the dish tasted of my childhood than she answered tit for tat, 'Mé oui, méoui, c'é du bon hachis d'boulettes d'z'orignal à la mode du pays.' ('But of course, it's made of ground moose meat made in the traditional manner.').

To be reminded of one's language and origins through taste and smell is a common experience for all minorities. European travellers' accounts of the West, Oregon, Louisiana, Acadia or the original Canada all contain tales of unexpected meetings with the missing link, always presented as isolated events or spicy anecdotes about one visitor or another and never forming a coherent whole. Yet, these chance meetings crop up all the time. Rarely do accounts of explorations in North America fail to stumble on a Native in *Canayen* clothing or vice-versa. Such adventures are always described with astonishment at having experienced such an extraordinary encounter. See, for example, this account by Père de Smet, the Belgian Jesuit of the Rockies and of Oregon, of his 1845 mission:

> After walking a month, I arrived at the source of the Columbia (the great river of Orégon [Ourigan]). I hardly expected to find there the possibility of exercising the holy ministry. But is there any place anywhere that the Canadiens have not penetrated? The king who reigns in this solitary land is a brave *habitant* named Morigeon de Saint-Martin (en Canada), who left his homeland 26 years ago. His palace is built of 13 moose skins and, to use his words, contains enough rooms to lodge his household, that is, his wife and his seven children and all their modest possessions; he is free to hold court (to build his lodge) anywhere he wishes without anyone coming to dispute his right to do so. His sceptre is a beaver trap; his law his rifle; one on his arm, one on his back, he visits, one after the other, his numerous subjects, the beaver, the otter, the muskrat, the marten, the bear, the caribou, the moose, the sheep, the mountain goat, the black-tailed deer, as well as its cousin the red-tailed. All, if the law reaches them, pay tribute in meat and skins. Surrounded by so many earthly delights, peaceable proprietor of all the granite castles with which nature has

embellished his domain, solitary lord of these majestic mountains whose snowy peaks pierce the clouds, Morigeon does not forget his Christian duty. Every day, evening and morning, he can be observed in the midst of his little family on their knees piously reciting their prayers. For many years, he had ardently desired to meet a priest; as soon as he knew of my arrival, he hastened to obtain for his wife and children the singular blessing of baptism.

This favour was accorded them the day of the nativity of the Holy Virgin, as well as to the children of three Indian families which follow him as he moves about. Here again, the holy sacrifice of sacred mass was offered for the first time. Morigeon drew close to the holy table. In memory of so many blessings, a large cross was driven into the ground at a place which we called Plain of the Nativity.

I cannot leave my brave Canadien without making honourable mention of his cooking. The first dish which he offered me was a stew made from two bear paws. An entire porcupine placed upon a spit then appeared; then a large pot was placed in the midst of the guests and each one selected the desired morsel. And what a choice! Pieces of buffalo and moose, beaver tails, partridge, turtledove, rabbit … something for every taste. (Recounted in Tassé, 1978, pp. xxii–iv)

At this point I should mention Old King Boliou (Vieux Roi Beaulieu), self-proclaimed chief, living with seven wives and seven families in an arm of the Salt River (*rivière de sel*) beside Great Slave Lake,[12] whose entire tribe was descended from a common ancestor. With the appearance of the first missionary, they at once fell to their knees and the Indianised *Canadien* automatically became a perfectly tamed Catholic once more. I sometimes wonder whether the beaver, the muskrat and the bear were also baptised at the same ceremony. It is this type of individual that attracts Francis Parkman, who admiringly describes the versatility of his guide, Henri Chatillon, in *The Oregon Trail*. After a gruelling wilderness crossing lasting five or six months, Chatillon is able, within a few minutes, to become a man of perfect urbanity, a prototype of characters expounded in the nascent literature of the US, such as the works of James Fenimore Cooper and James Michener's *Centennial*.

What should we do with the wealth of information that flies in the face of North America's official history? This includes the history of the region which, under the name of Québec, has chosen to dissociate itself from a glorious past, without which it would never have existed. There are two choices here for the *Canadiens*, transformed into people of Québec. Will they merely deposit

---

12 The prudish British adopted this name from Petit Lac des Mamelles (Small Lake of Big Tits), given to it by the Dené, according to legend.

this richness in the bottom of a drawer reserved for anecdotes to be used as footnotes by anthropologists who amuse themselves with such history? Or will they make them one of the essential elements of a supplanted memory begging for recognition?

*

In the 1930s, a book appeared in New York and London which would become a classic, Grace Lee Nute's *The Voyageur*:

> It is time to write the story of the voyageur. His canoe has long since vanished from the northern waters; his red cap [tuque] is seen no more, a bright spot against the blue of Lake Superior; his sprightly French conversation, punctuated with inimitable gesture, his exaggerated courtesy, his incurable romanticism, his songs, and his superstitions are gone. [But] In certain old books and in many unpublished manuscripts, he still lives in the books of so many explorers' account.

> From their pages peals the laughter of a gay-hearted, irrepressible race; over night waters floats the plaintive song of canoe-man, swelled periodically in the chorus by the voices of his lusty mates; portage path and campfire, foaming rapids and placid fir-fringed lake, shallow winding stream and broad expanse of inland sea, whitewalled cottage of Québec hamlet and frowning pickets of north-west post ... though he is one of the most colourful figures in the history of a great continent, the voyageur remains unknown to all but a few ...

> Probably the greatest contribution of the voyageur to the development of the continent was the knowledge of the wilderness and its ways that he put freely and with no hope of recognition at the disposal of the great explorers of the West and North. (Nute, 1955, pp. vii, viii and 227)

With no hope of recognition! But with a wink of fate to escape extinction, the *Canadien voyageur* stands at the edge of a plateau, on a river's ramparts or at the confluence of oblivion, but he is incognito everywhere in the heart of America.

It is incontrovertible, continues Grace Lee Nute, that practically every exploratory trip made after the British conquest employed *voyageurs*. Everyone who travelled in the north west before the days of the railroad sooner or later used French-Canadian [sic] *voyageurs* or their half-breed descendants to paddle their canoes, drive their dogs, lead their packhorses, choose their routes, or guide their York boats. And the sledge dogs of the Yukon and Alaska in the far north? If they don't bark in *canayen*, they receive their orders in *canayen* — *mach/mach/mush* — from guides unaware that this word is derived from *march/mach-mach*, the old pronunciation of *marcher* (to walk), used to address domestic animals on the Coste-du-Sud where I write these words.[13] But none of these *voyageurs*, more skilled with axe than pen, will ever tell their version of history. Nor will they recount the jokes and amusements they shared around the campfire. Yet the *voyageurs* represent our history, which can come alive from the toponyms they coined on their travels, without for a moment realising this would be the inheritance they left us. The intersection of Franco-America's geography, history and culture is clearly demonstrated in the names they bestowed on the places where they stayed and the physical features they saw. Their legacy sings out in such nomenclature as: Rivière Maligne; Portage de la Racine d'Ours; Demi-charge de Chétauque; Arrêt du Pemmican; Anse de la Dérouine; Décharge de la Queue-de-Rat; Baie de la Carotte-à-Moreau; Rapide de l'Équerre; Portage la Loche (Methy Portage); Lac de l'Anus-de-l'Onde; Grande Isle des Fouettes-Sec; Rivière-aux-Embarras; Baie de la Bête-Grise; Roche Trempe-à-l'Eau; Bivouac de la Tripe-de-Roche; Portage du Rocher-Plumé; Baie du Colle-au-Vent; and Montée du Wattape. The lyrical inventions of *Canadiens* on their travels, these names were transcribed by the French and adopted by the English, often with radical transformations. When Rivières-aux-Embarras is changed to Zumbrota River, it is difficult to discern its original name initially inscribed on the 'skin' of the territory — a century after the French had themselves laid down a layer of toponyms whose meaning has been forgotten. To whom exactly do all these names belong, if not to the patrimony of the hemisphere in its entirety?

And what is the message of the following names deposited a century before upon the 'skin' of Canada: Ohahaudion; Khiondakouananiautonon; Eachirion; Inchere; Chokande; Aouentalouaenronon; Enrié; Lac des Nipisiriens Skenchoronon; and Lac des Eaux-de-Mer? These toponymic fragments were drawn on animal skin that was part of the booty pillaged after the capitulation of Québec. It is puzzling to examine a document (Figure 3) bearing titles in French and English: 'Carte anonyme de la Nouvelle-France, circa 1640' and 'The Huron Map' respectively. It might be said 'there are your codices, there is your genesis … your founding poem', so founding, in fact, that one cannot even understand their terms as most of the place names have never been translated! This confusion is reinforced when skirting 'The Huron Map' between Le Nouveau-Mexic, La Virginie, La Nouvelle-Flandre, La Nouvelle-Angleterre, Lacadie surrounding la Nation du Pétun, la Nation des Gens de Mer ou Puants, les Gens de Feu, Nation du Chat, les Iroquois, les Algom-Quins and les Montaignets. To whom exactly do all these names and accompanying stories, forever silent, belong? To all those who have forgotten them and who

13   The Coste-du-Sud lies on the south shore of the St Lawrence between Montmagny and
     Saint-Jean-Port-Joli. The author's home is in Saint-Michel-de-Bellechasse at the heart of this
     region.

Figure 3: 'Carte Anonyme de la Nouvelle France circa 1640'/'The Huron Map'.

clumsily attempt to pronounce them? Or to all those who dream them and seek to recapture their essence for want of meaning?

*

And so, what is our heritage? The first words of *Nord-Amérique* with meanings have vanished forever. They were coined by the *coureur de bois*, then revised by the French Jesuits and renewed again by England, which exhibited them in its

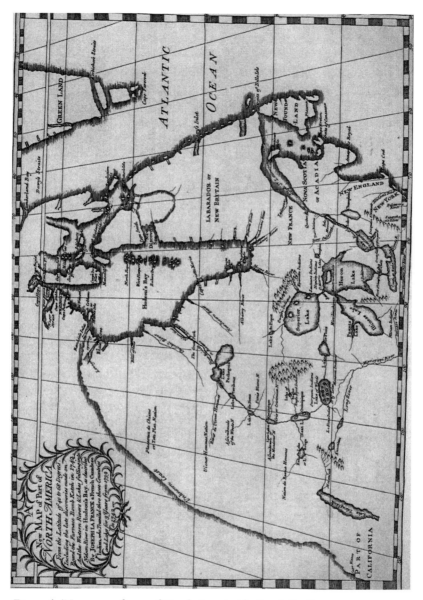

Figure 4: 'New map of part of North America' by Joseph La France.

museums. Words like Ohahaudion and Khiondakouananiautonon are in quest
of reincarnation, but have to be left in a state of semi-survival only on an old
map that is itself a historical relic. What else can one do apart from allowing
them to mix with all the other words that emanated from within the continent
exactly one century later as described by Joseph La France, 'a French Canadese

Indian, who Travaled thro those Countries and Lakes for 3 Years from 1739 to 1742'. The document reprinted here in Figure 4 is by some distance the first *Canadien*-produced literary text to originate from the homeland and not via a European vision. However, it cannot be found in any anthology for it is perceived neither as a poem nor as the accurate record of an apocryphal author carrying half a continent in his head.

Joseph La France's adventure proves to be an odyssey comparable to those of the great navigators who plied the oceans, except that his was an 'earthly' sea. As for all those who tend to stigmatise its veracity,[14] they miss the significance of an illiterate *Métis* bearing a kingdom upon his shoulders and carrying an unwritten geography in his pouch. This man, who was neither Joseph nor La France — names brutally imposed to replace his given *Canayen-Solteux* name, now lost forever — can be visualised standing in the midst of North America with a secret *Nord-Amérique* in his arms. A man who, standing on tiptoe in his moccasins, surveys the Arctic and the Pacific with one glance, which then sweeps beyond the Mississippi to the confines of the Shining Sea (Tahuglauk).

His life's journey and the joys of his travels will never be found in writings destined for princes, prelates or kings. His discoveries will never be attributed to him because he is himself an ambulatory and unexpected discovery. Far from being a simple cartographic transposition, his word constitutes one of the first geographic sagas left to us by a *Métis Franco*, one it seems no one dared to recognise. Marching through a network of rivers and a maze of lakes, the *Canadese* Indian built a lodge near a *coulée*, set up his table on an erratic block deposited by a geologic thaumaturge or an indulgent or benevolent Manitou. The words 'en roulant ma boule en roulant' which he wrote on the parchment are his only testament for posterity:

> between Lake de Pluis and Lake du Pique,
> Lake Pachegoia and Great Lake Ouinipique
> the Plascotez de Chiens and the Nation of Beaux Hommes,
> Lovegrove's opening and the River Oulaouas,
> Trois Rivières and the Epenitts Indians,
> the Vieux Hommes Nation and Puants Lake,
> the Ouafsi Indians and the Sauteurs Indians,
> Michipikoton and Missilimakinac
> Cape Blanco and the Straits of Canseaux,
> the Bay of Sakinac and Lake Frontenac ...
> the River Saint-Laurence and the Unknown Coast
> Part of California and the New Found Land!

14 'The La France map is more a cartographic curiosity than a competent survey': Armstrong, 1982, entry no. 23.

how many Manitouves,
how many love stories,
how many *chasses-galeries*,
how many forgotten crossings,
how many founding bivouacs
stand out at the edge of the dream?

*

And so ... how to conclude?
We have just travelled through an entire continent and through three centuries.
All peoples of the Americas seek their evanescent origin
and the time has come to decipher the story of the *voyageur* ...
to add a chapter shedding a new light on the pathways of oblivion
But the time has also come to rewrite the history
of a *Nord-Amérique* concealed by North America
The time has come to bring to life the soul of a *Métis* land.

A city has celebrated her 400th birthday
under the name of Québec
but she is an unread book
written by a forgotten land,
a mysterious hand and
a vanished secret named Canada
from whence has emerged the whole of *Nord-Amérique*.

And we *Canadiens*, sons of an illiterate heritage
are in search of illumination.
And at the end, all we have to get there
are hundreds of cartographic documents — maps —
deposited around the land and drawn by Europe.
And so we are left with blurred traces
and the raw memory of melted snow.

To feel the orographic palpitations of a continent is one thing,
but to feel the overleaf of history wiped clean is another.
The time has come to bring to life
the transcript of an oral geography.

Québec, soul city of the Americas...
Québec, a name and a call.
The name of an America that is neither French nor British
the call of a half-illegitimate America asking for recognition
Québec, a French Native promise lingering
half-way between dusk and twilight
Québec, ultimate dream of the Americas.

REFERENCES

Armstrong, Joe C.W. (1982) *From Sea unto Sea. Art and Discovery Maps of Canada* (Scarborough and Toronto: Fleet/Lester and Orphen Dennys Books).

Blevins, Winfred (1993) *Dictionary of the American West* (New York: Facts on File), p. xi and p. 226.

Brasser, Ted. J. (1985) 'In search of métis art', in Jacqueline Peterson and Jennifer Brown, *Being and Becoming Métis in North America* (Winnipeg: The University of Manitoba Press), pp. 221–9.

Braz, Albert (2003) *The False Traitor: Louis Riel in Canadian Culture* (Toronto/Buffalo/London: University of Toronto Press).

Braz, Albert (2005) 'North of America: Racial hybridity and Canada's (non) place in inter-American discourse', *Comparative American Studies,* Vol. 3, No. 1 (March), pp. 79–88.

Franklin, Wayne (1979) *Discoverers, Explorers, Settlers: The Diligent Writers of Early America* (Chicago: University of Chicago Press).

Havard, Gilles and Cécile Vidal (2007) 'Making New France New Again', *Common-Place,* vol. 7, no. 4, www.common-place.org (July).

Hayes, Derek (2002) *Historical Atlas of Canada* (Vancouver/Seattle: Douglas and McIntyre Ltd and University of Washington Press).

Louder, Dean and Eric Waddell (2007) *Du continent perdu à l'archipel retrouvé, Le Québec et l'Amérique française* (Québec: Les Presses de l'Université Laval [1983]).

Morisset, Jean (1984) 'À la recherche de la langue errante … In Quest of the Couteau-Jaune Frenchy', *The AFLA Review* [Alaska Foreign Language Association Newsletter] vol. 5, no. 2 (Fairbanks: University of Alaska).

Morisset, Jean (1986) 'En quête de l'Amérique amériquaine. L'Identité amériquaine, l'Amérique française et l'idée d'Amérique latine', in *Actes du 45e congrès international des américanistes* (Bogotá, Colombie).

Morisset, Jean (1987a) 'L'autre à travers le même ou L'Amérique française à l'encontre de la Franco-Amérique', in *Écrits du Canada français* no. 60 (Montréal), pp. 87–98.

Morisset, Jean (1987b) 'Le français au verso des Amériques ou les Amériques et le français', in *Actes du 8è Congrès national des professeurs de français du Brésil, Revista Elos – Número Especial 2: Le français et les Amériques* (Porto Alegre), pp. 32–40.

Morisset, Jean (1988) 'L'appel géographique et la parenthèse du Canadien gris-et-sauvage', in Gilles Thérien (ed.), *Les figures de l'Indien*, Cahiers du Département d'Études Littéraires, no. 9 (Montréal: Université du Québec), pp. 345–52.

Morisset, Jean (1992a) 'An America that Knows no Name: Postscript to a Quincentenary Celebration', in Dean Louder and Eric Waddell (eds.), *French America: Mobility, Identity and Minority Experience Across the Continent* (Bâton Rouge: Louisiana State University Press), pp. 337–47.

Morisset, Jean (1992b) 'Paroles de Québécois traduites du Tchippewayan et autres dialectiques géographiques', *Recherches Amérindiennes au Québec*, vol. XXII, nos. 2–3, pp. 117–22.

Morisset, Jean (1996) 'The way I understand it ... or trying to find a place to pray in peace'. A spontaneous conversation at the Akwesasne (Québec-New York-Ontario) Indian reserve with Feu Gesso alias KaroniaKeson (unpublished), 17 pp.

Morisset, Jean (ed. and trans.) (1997) *Mathias Carvalho* (1886), *Louis Riel: Poèmes amériquains* (Québec: éditions Trois-Pistoles).

Morisset, Jean (2001) 'Une vie en translation ou le vertige et la gloire d'être Franco', in Dean Louder, Jean Morisset and Eric Waddell (eds.), *Espaces de vie, espaces de rêve. Visages et visions de la Franco-Amérique.* (Québec: Éditions du Septentrion), pp. 285–313.

Morisset, Jean (2008) 'À la recherche du Canada errant ou le chant de l'impossible', *Les Cahiers de l'idiotie*, vol. 1, no. 1 (Ottawa), pp.195–246.

Nute, Grace Lee (1955) *The Voyageur* (Saint-Paul: Minnesota Historical Society, [1931]).

Tassé, Joseph (1978) *Les Canadiens de l'Ouest. Tome premier* (Montréal: Cie d'Imprimerie canadienne).

Vallée, Jacques (1973) *Tocqueville au Bas-Canada* (Montréal: Éditions du Jour).

3
THE SPACES OF QUEBEC CITY

Bill Marshall

Overlooking the St Lawrence in Québec City is one of Québec province's key foundational sites, the Parc des Champs de Bataille (the Plains of Abraham, named after someone who grazed his sheep there). It was here that British troops under General Wolfe, having scaled the 53-metre cliff above the L'Anse-au-Foulon cove, defeated the Marquis de Montcalm's forces in 1759, a victory that effectively brought New France into the British Empire. When the nationalist intellectual Jacques Godbout returned to these sites for his 1996 documentary, *Le Sort de l'Amérique*, he was surprised to find himself in agreement with the assessment of historian Laurier L. Lapierre in *1759 Battle for Canada*, published four years earlier, as to the national identity of the *Canadiens* who had either fought the British in Québec, or were simply spectators to the battle (Lapierre, 1992). The great secret is that they were not or were no longer French and no 'major' identity was lost here.[1] Jocelyn Létourneau is one of the leading contemporary Québec (and Québec City) intellectuals to articulate this minor, 'in-between', even creolised reality of French-Canadian and then Québec culture, a reality characterised by alliances rather than with filiation vis-à-vis France:

> Ni désireux d'assimiler totalement leur devenir à celui de l'Amérique
> ni soucieux de rompre complètement avec leurs attaches françaises,
> mais se déployant allègrement dans le lacis des deux continentalités;
> refusant tout à la fois la perspective de l'autochtonisation (cesser d'être
> Européen en Amérique) et celle de la reproduction à l'identique (rester
> Européen en Amérique), mais (re)composant leur stock de références dans
> l'entrecroisement des deux civilisations, les Canadiens, avec le temps, se
> créent graduellement une identité.

---

1 Godbout's unsettling experience continues when he visits the descendants of Montcalm and Wolfe, and rather than discovering the expected elderly, seemingly out-of-time French aristocrat, finds that the BBC news reporter Andrew Burroughs is 'beaucoup plus proche de nous'.

This part of his analysis continues with a Deleuzean flourish:

> En fait, la Nouvelle-France n'est pas un lieu où l'univocité de l'agir et du
> dessein prend racine. La société qui s'élève — appelons-la canadienne
> — se situe au contraire comme dans une ligne de fuite par rapport à
> elle-même, ce qu'expriment bien les couples sédentarité/nomadisme,
> francité/américanité et tradition/envie d'altérité qui la définissent
> fondamentalement. (Létourneau, 2006, p. 24)

In my own work, I have sought to trace what I call the 'national-allegorical'
tension, between centrifugal/centripetal, or deterritorialising/reterritorialising
forces that characterise the texts of Québec nationhood. But what happens
when we look at Québec's national capital, with its massive, seemingly
centripetal identity investments?

The foundational sites are one part of this complex story. In the early 21st
century, the population of Québec City, as defined by its official boundaries,
is around 170,000. However, its urban area, that is the zone of continuous
population density surrounding it, contains 613,000 people (placing it tenth
among French-speaking cities in the world and the largest in this study).
According to Statistics Canada, moreover, its metropolitan area including, for
example, the town of Lévis on the south shore of the St Lawrence, exceeded
700,000 in 2005. This disproportionate gap, in which Québec City leaps
from 22nd to seventh place in Canadian population rankings when urban
area rather than strict city limits is taken into account, is approached only by
Vancouver (0.5 to 1.8 million, moving from eighth to third). The explanation
— history and topography (Vancouver was founded on a peninsula and
developed between a sea inlet and a major river) — holds true for Québec City,
with 'French Atlantic' twists involving geopolitics and the changing destiny of
francophone North America.[2]

Québec City can be viewed as a series of concentric circles, more so even
than a typical western city radiating outward from its central, foundational
and pre-industrial or pre-modern core — a feature especially, although not
uniquely, typical of Europe.[3] What is known as 'Vieux Québec' consists of
two entities, the Haute Ville/Upper Town and the Basse Ville/Lower Town

2   Following its election in 2003, the provincial Liberal government set in motion the
     separation of municipalities that had been 'fused together' by its Parti Québécois predecessor.
     However, local consultation produced only two 'défusions' in the Québec City area, those of
     L'Ancienne-Lorette and St-Augustin-Desmaures.

3   Indeed this is one of the concluding descriptions in one of the main recent historical
     accounts of the city: 'La vie sociale et culturelle de Québec se présente comme une série de
     cercles concentriques qui se touchent parfois sans jamais se rencontrer' (Hare *et al.*, 1987, p.
     306).

(or, to distinguish it from another part of the city, the Vieux Port/Old Port), which formed the basis of the 1608 foundation and its aftermath. This latter narrow strip of land, later expanded through reclamation from the river, lies between the St Lawrence, the estuary of its tributary the St Charles, and an 80-metre-high cliff, and is where Samuel de Champlain built his first *habitation*. Evolving from a *quartier populaire* of artisans and workers in the 18th century into an important financial and warehouse district in the 19th century, the section which is slightly distanced from the main tourist hub reinvented itself in the late 20th century as a district of cultural industries and loft living. The site of the first garden, the Haute Ville on the high plateau overlooking the river, is where monumental building work took place during the French regime, housing political and ecclesiastical authority principally in a Governor's Palace, Cathedral, Seminary, Jesuit College, and Ursulines Convent (the Basse-Ville was too small for such structures, apart from the church of Notre-Dame-des-Victoires, built in 1688–90, but even that is modest in size). The Haute Ville is surrounded by almost completely intact city walls, enhanced and perfected by the British in 1832 in the wake of the War of 1812 with the US. *Intra* these *muros* — their frontier effect exaggerated on the western side by the intact *non aedificandi* zone, now a wide esplanade — where enemy troops had to approach without cover, the urban space is dominated by a hotel, the Château Frontenac. The other element of the Upper Town is what exists beyond these walls: just outside, but at a slightly higher elevation, lie the *hôtel du parlement* or National Assembly (renamed as such in 1968 as a symbolical means of surpassing mere provincial parliament status, as created by Canadian Confederation in 1867) and a host of other buildings (the highest of which is the 32-storey Edifice G), housing ministries and *fonctionnaires* dedicated to the administration of Québec. The town *extra muros* thus continues the theme of authority and power westwards and was where wealthier or at least more middle-class sections of the population elected to live as the city expanded in the 19th century, with bourgeois dwellings — including many Victorian villas built by the British elites — lining the Grande Allée and the streets off it. The Saint-Jean Baptiste district just to the north, the site of a certain gay gentrification in the 1980s, takes this residential zone to the edge of the high plateau.

Gazing northwards at this point, the modern visitor is struck by two sights which complete the 'symbolic concentricity' of Québec's national capital, but which are in fact outside their field of vision and the standard tourist itinerary. Immediately below lies another Basse Ville, between the cliff face and the St Charles river or just beyond it, comprising the working-class districts of Saint Roch and Saint Sauveur. And beyond that, seemingly stretching as far as the Laurentian mountains and ski resorts 25 kilometres away, is a

North American suburbia of freeways, shopping malls and detached houses (among these suburbs is the Huron reservation, the village of Wendake, still administered under the structures of the 1877 Indian Act, with 'status Indians' enjoying exclusive residential rights, their own police force, and tax breaks — an important commercial element is cigarette retailing — in exchange for an originary subaltern status). In fact, the Old City is surrounded by such suburbs: Sainte-Foy to the west, where the main campus of Laval University is now located; Beauport to the north-east; St Romuald, Charny and Lévis-Lauzon to the south. Car ownership in Québec City, at 49.5 per cent, is on a par with that to be found in other suburban zones in the province and far exceeds that in Montréal (35.3 per cent). And since, according to the 2001 Canadian census, the population of Québec City is now 96 per cent francophone (compared to 67 per cent for Montréal), that North American suburbia takes place exclusively in French (already by the 1930s the French geographer Raoul Blanchard had noted how this suburbia had reconfigured the city, 'Québec devient une ville de plaine avec des annexes sur la colline' (Blanchard, 1935, p. 292)).

This brief overview of the city's demographic and spatial configurations has immediate and evident implications for an exploration of the relationship between space, place and meaning. For one thing, the concentric circles speak to a history of transformation, not only of the territory but of what it means or meant to be French, *Canadien*, French-Canadian, Québécois. Moreover, they suggest ways of understanding the symbolic use to which Québec City has been put in terms of both governmental strategy and cultural representation. Let us first explore a history of the meanings of Québec City as generated by its spatial characteristics, a history that can be grouped under four interrelated headings: origin, port and fortress; topography, hierarchy and power; the differentiation from Montréal; and questions of heritage and tourism.

Origin, Port and Fortress

Québec City's dual function as port and fortress, of openness and enclosure, forms the deep structure of all its representations. The site, known as 'kebec' in Algonquin ('where the river narrows'), marks the point where the St Lawrence begins to open up into its estuary, but its width here is just one kilometre, with very deep water offshore and a convenient harbour at the mouth of the St Charles by the narrow area (exaggerated by Champlain on maps) that was the original Basse Ville. Although a thousand kilometres from the Atlantic, ocean-going ships can dock here, making Québec City for several centuries a principal European gateway to the North American interior. Coupled with a hinterland rich in forests and furs and a strong agricultural potential on lowlands between the Canadian Shield to the north and the Appalachians to the south, it was an obvious centre for French settlement and trade. Moreover, the heights above gave Champlain a commanding position from which to observe and police shipping on the river at a time when he was seeking to enforce a fur monopoly. As Blanchard noted, 'Une porte, c'est-à-dire l'ouverture par où circulent les échanges de toute la région avec l'extérieur, et en même temps le chambranle qui permet d'interdire le passage de toute activité hostile' (Blanchard, 1935, p. 165). On the other hand, the port suffered some disadvantages, most notably being closed between November and May because of ice, making it initially more difficult — than, say, Acadia, directly on the ocean — to integrate fully into a French Atlantic economy. Triangular trade was limited: mostly during Jean Talon's tenure as Intendant (1665–72), ships left Québec City in October laden with cereals (and later with the wooden barrels used to transport sugar to France), arriving in the Caribbean in December, returning to France in the spring and then to Québec in July. Prevailing winds from the south-west or north-east could disrupt navigation in the era of sail, making it difficult to enter the Gulf of St Lawrence and sometimes forcing ships to head southwards to the Caribbean instead.

Nonetheless, Québec City was the major hub of New France's commerce within the French mercantilist system, receiving manufactured goods from the metropole and exporting wooden planks, fish oil, salmon and cod, cereal products such as flour and biscuits when harvests were good, and of course furs, which constituted 70 per cent of the total value. The port also traded locally along the St Lawrence, with the French concession of Plaisance in Newfoundland and then the fortress of Louisbourg on Cape Breton Island in present-day Nova Scotia. These Atlantic connections included the networks of merchants and *armateurs* from Bordeaux, Rouen and especially La Rochelle, whose agents either settled in Québec City or spent part of the year there. Typical itineraries are those of the cousins François Havy (1709–66) and Jean Lefebvre (1714–60), who came to Québec City in the 1730s as representatives of the Rouen shipping company, Dugard et Cie. When the latter abandoned its interests in New France a decade later due to ship losses, Havy and Lefebvre began trading independently in furs, seal and other products with France and the Caribbean.

The Seven Years War and the fall of New France to the British disrupted this triangular initiative. The two cousins consequently sought to base themselves in La Rochelle, but Lefebvre's death at sea in 1760 hampered this redevelopment. The port of Québec City, like the wider territory of New France, initially had to operate within the relatively limited economic parameters of the new colonial order. As a standard historical study has explained:

> Partie intégrante d'une économie coloniale peu diversifiée et d'un marché
> exigu, Québec se tourne vers l'Atlantique pour faire sa fortune. Mais
> saccadée de temps forts et faibles de courte durée, l'économie maritime de
> la ville n'a jamais le capital ni, souvent, le loisir d'établir des assises stables,

génératrices de croissance. (Hare *et al.*, 1987, p. 103)

British merchants took over the city's commercial activities, as the former New France was integrated after 1763 into British imperial networks of trade and capital accumulation. However, the late 18th and early 19th centuries witnessed a fresh wave of expansion.

The disruption of the American Revolutionary War was followed by geopolitical events which directly and indeed spectacularly benefited Québec City. The most important of these developments was the renewal of trade between Britain and the US from 1796, and the outbreak of the Napoleonic Wars in Europe, which compelled Britain to seek its timber from sources other than its traditional suppliers in Scandinavia. In 1807–11, Québec exports of blocks and planks increased 650 per cent, and in 1806–14 shipments of wood products of all kinds increased by 375 per cent. This gave rise to an extensive logging and wood-processing industry in the hinterland and massively increased shipbuilding activity in the area itself. Indeed, the two biggest wooden ships of the 19th century — the 3,700-ton *Columbus* and 5,888-ton *Baron Renfrew* — were built in Québec City, in 1824 and 1825 respectively. By 1830, Québec City was the third most important port in North America — after New York and New Orleans — in terms of the amount of goods traded. By 1850, it saw 1,300 ship movements a year and in the Basse Ville, in particular, the intermingling of sailors, *draveurs* and immigrants produced a cosmopolitan atmosphere. The result was a significant expansion of the city's population from 8,000 in 1800, a level only slightly higher than during French rule, to 20,000 in 1832 and 60,000 by 1860.

Québec City as fortress and military centre also dates from Champlain. The first *habitation* had palisades, ditches and a drawbridge and in 1620 the first fort — the château St Louis — was built on the promontory above. Against the British in 1629 and 1759, the city's much lauded defences proved completely ineffective, of course, and in the early years the fortress served no more of a purpose than as a refuge against attackers. But the tension between port and fortress, openness and closure, eloquently expresses the relationship between the French and the local native populations, for Québec City was a pre-eminent 'contact zone' of European imperial history, 'the space of colonial encounters, the space in which peoples geographically separated come into contact with each other and establish ongoing relations, usually involving conditions of coercion, radical inequality, and intractable conflict' (Pratt, 1992, pp. 6–7).

During his first winter in the area in 1535–6, Jacques Cartier's relationships with the natives at their settlement at Stadacona (which no longer existed when the French returned in 1608) were characterised by dependency but also mistrust to the point of paranoia. As is well known, European evocations of the North American native peoples were profoundly mediated by their own Mediterranean-centred and instrumentalist agendas. Sixty years later, Champlain in his writings and drawings assessed the natives on the basis of their being either *errants* or *arrestes* and sought to impose the latter, sedentary and agricultural way of life on populations which would thus be easier to control. Such mappings are echoed in the writings of the Recollect friar, Gabriel Sagard, 'Je tiens les Hurons, et autres peuples Sédentaires, comme la Noblesse: les nations Algoumequines pour les Bourgeois, et les autres Sauvages de deçà comme Montagnets et Canadiens, les villageois et pauvres du pays.' (Courville & Caron, 2001, p. 42) Indeed, the area was a meeting point of various native groups: the hunter-gathering Montagnais and Algonquins; the Hurons who arrived from the Great Lakes area as part of fur-trading networks; and, dominating the area south of the St Lawrence, the Iroquois, enemy to both the French and more northerly native groups, who eventually allied themselves with the English.

The small number of French settlers forced a dependency on native groups for knowledge and on the surface a more co-operative approach than existed elsewhere, but the devalorisation of native cultures went hand in hand with a valorisation for the French alone of the land and its resources and the beginning of the native peoples' subaltern status. Coinciding with the Counter-Reformation and Cardinal Richelieu's national offensive in France itself, religious surveillance and authority were additionally stimulated in Québec City by the native presence (which increased significantly after the destruction of Huronia by the Iroquois in 1649 — in 1650, 400 Hurons were living in cabins near the Hôtel-Dieu), with a rack and pillory visible in front of the settlement's parish church after 1632. This paranoia about the Iroquois impelled a series of witchhunts and exorcisms, with six natives burned at the stake in the 17th century and a Beauport miller executed for witchcraft in 1661. This policing and surveillance thus coexisted uneasily with the developing cultures of hybridity forged by younger French men setting forth on the fur trading networks, the *coureurs de bois* and *voyageurs*. While the city hosted some native populations, these were in the main kept at a distance, only coming into contact with Europeans in 'neutral' spaces such as the Jesuit mission, built just outside (at Sillery) in 1637, which is still intact today.

Topography, Hierarchy and Power

Raoul Blanchard was neither the first nor last commentator to remark upon the homology between physical and social elevation in Québec City, 'Manifestement l'altitude est en raison directe de la richesse; moins on est à l'aise, plus on s'éloigne des hauteurs' (Blanchard, 1935, p. 266). As early as the beginning of the 18th century, the Haute Ville was mainly inhabited by a bourgeoisie emanating from the administrative, military and religious apparatuses of the

French state, as well as from commerce (mainly that of services), who owned most of the city's property. Most of the artisans, shopkeepers and workers lived in the Basse Ville, where shipyards, tanning, hat and shoe factories had sprung up by 1666. The growth in this work populace impelled the expansion of the city in 1752 into the Saint-Roch *faubourg*; this became the most populous district of the city by 1819 and was fully integrated within the municipal boundaries in 1833.

British rule perpetuated the Haute Ville/Basse Ville hierarchy, with the former dominated by British administrative and military personnel and a British bourgeoisie after 1760 (the Conquest saw the departure of most of the French elites except the clergy). The new Anglican cathedral of the Holy Trinity was consecrated in 1804 on the site of a Recollect convent and church which had burned down in 1796. Even within the Haute Ville, a certain ethno-spatial configuration emerged, with the British occupying the best properties, between the rues Saint-Louis and Saint-Jean (Hare *et al.*, 1987, pp. 153–4). The Basse Ville, and particularly Saint-Roch, became the terrain of the city's industrialisation in the 19th century, increasing the fragmentation of the city's space and the perception of such. At the same time urban expansion led to the creation of a string of middle-class 'villas' to the west of the Haute Ville, along the chemins Saint-Louis and Sainte-Foy, often with river views and sited in verdant grounds, although they later gave way, either to more modest cottage-like constructions influenced by Romanticism, or, faced with demographic expansion, to large terraced dwellings that grew up along the Grande Allée.

The most striking construction in the Haute Ville during the 19th century was, of course, the luxurious Château Frontenac hotel, the first section of which was completed in 1893 on the site of the French colonial château Saint-Louis, which had burned down in 1834 and been cleared by the Governor-General, Lord Dufferin, in 1879 in order to complete the monumental boardwalk overlooking the St Lawrence. The hotel was designed by an American architect, Bruce Price, for the Canadian Pacific Railway and then, headed by Sir William Van Horne, took the style — although built in Scottish brick — of a Renaissance French château, with many references to the Comte de Frontenac (Governor-General of New France 1672–82, recalled to battle against the Iroquois during the 1690s). Different suites paid homage to various constituencies: the *habitant* with French-Canadian artisanry and motifs, a Chinese (for Pacific) room and a Dutch room (for van Horne, Amsterdam financiers). In the 1920s, the great Champlain dining room was created, with ceiling panels alternating the British rose and lion and the French griffon and *fleur-de-lys* (the latter also appeared on the door handles). Arguably, this duality expressed the ambiguous identity issues lived by the francophone bourgeoisie that was now poised to dominate the Haute Ville and the city itself. As two Québec historians recently observed:

> Bien que durant le premier quart du XXe siècle la bourgeoisie d'origine
> francophone vive selon le modèle d'une haute bourgeoisie majoritairement
> d'origine anglo-saxonne, ne tente-t-elle pas de se distinguer de cette
> dernière grâce à son caractère français, référant à des racines parfois plus
> mythiques que réelles? (Courville & Garon, 2001, p. 319)

In addition, the nexus of topography, hierarchy and financial/cultural power embodied by this most iconic of Québec City's buildings was enlarged by its international dimension, that of a place open to the world, not only to well-heeled, largely American tourists, but in the staging of conferences such as the Churchill-Roosevelt encounters in 1943 and 1944.

In the immediate postwar era, Québec City was dominated by traditional *notables* and inhabited by low-paid industrial workers and civil servants yoked to a conservative provincial regime (that of Premier Maurice Duplessis, 1944–59) that had scant interest in an active, interventionist state. However, the Quiet Revolution of the 1960s marked a massive change in the role of government. The number of civil servants mushroomed in 20 years, from 15,000 to 45,000. The emergence of this new technocratic middle class, despite — or because of — its progressive intentions that favoured the interests of Québec's francophones, in fact perpetuated many of the city's spatial divisions. This was illustrated by more than just the office skyscrapers of the parliament district: a closer look at the evolution and meaning of the Saint-Roch district is also revealing on this score.

Both Marc Grignon and Lucie K. Morisset have done valuable work not simply on the history of the district, but on its relationship to the image — and its representation in images — of the city as a whole (Grignon, 1999; Morisset, 1999; see also Grignon, 1995 and Morisset & Noppen, 1995). Throughout the period of French rule, illustrations of Québec City were governed by a remarkable stability of visual conventions. For example, an engraving published in Claude-Charles Le Roy de La Potherie's *Histoire de l'Amérique septentrionale* (1722) — and much imitated throughout the 18th century — captures the city from an observation point to the east, on the St Lawrence but higher than water level, the view framing it from the Cap aux Diamants on the left to the mouth of the St Charles on the right. The ornamentality of the sailing ships in the foreground is confirmed by the clear view afforded above them towards the Haute Ville, its public buildings, spires and churches exaggeratedly visible. Grignon argues that this visibility was bound up with the conventions of royal and court power, via which an image of Québec was constructed in Europe and, reciprocally, that image — of what the monarch might himself have gazed upon — was assimilated by local elites. Québec City's status as the emanation and manifestation of royal power in New France was dependent on its representation as such (and this explains the comparative rarity at the time of images of Montréal).

In contrast, the period of British rule was marked by a multiplication of points of view, at first bound up with military agendas concerning strategy, topography and reportage (notably the 12 realist, non-triumphalist renditions of the devastated town made in 1761 by the British officer Richard Short), but also including notions of the picturesque and of the painter's subjectivity, as the viewpoint became explicit rather than abstract. This multiplication also meant therefore that views *from* the Haute Ville were now more common, preparing the way for Lord Dufferin's transformations. A good example is James Pattison Cockburn's *The Lower City of Québec, from the Parapet of the Upper City*, 1833. In general, British artists during the decades following the Conquest were at pains both to extend domestic notions of the picturesque to the new imperial domains, and also to emphasise, especially in the 1770s and 80s when policies such as the Québec Act worked to keep the *Canadiens* onside in the face of American rebellion, the social and political tranquility of the landscape. Typifying this perspective, James Peachey's *View of Quebec and the St Lawrence River* (1786) dwarfs the distant city on the hill with a bucolic foreground of livestock and civilians — peasants and strollers.[4]

Visual representations of the Saint Roch district in the Basse Ville, minimised thus during the French period, were late and sporadic. Indeed, in 1692 its Recollect monastery had been replaced by a general hospital housing the blind, the insane, the paralysed and the poor who could not dwell at the Hôtel-Dieu in town, so that the new *faubourg* — appropriately named after Saint Roch, patron saint of catastrophe and plague — became a place of banishment and was itself cast away from the city's self-image. When images of it did appear in the artistic domain, these tended to be part of what Morisset describes as a *regard descendant*. Typifying this, in Philip James Bainbrigge's *St Charles River seen from the Heights of St John's Gate*, painted in 1836, it is squeezed between the last buildings on the north side of the Haute Ville and the river and plain sweeping towards the Laurentians. The same is characteristic of Alexander Jamieson Russell's *St Rock's Suburb and the Roman Catholic Church*, painted in 1840. Indeed, the hierarchical division of both labour and aesthetics evident in the industrial character of Saint Roch had been underlined by the decision to build a cholera hospital there (a severe epidemic hit the city in 1832). The stigmatisation of the industrial city that was Saint Roch was crystallised first in literature by a visiting Englishwoman, Isabella Lucy Bird, in 1854 (Bird, 1966). By the 1890s, however, when the district had became more prosperous, with all the trappings of nascent North American consumerism such as department stores and tall buildings, new bird's eye views of the city began to place the district at the centre in order to attract future business. This provoked a virulent

4   For more on visual representations made during the early British period, see Parent, 2005, and Crowley, 2005..

reaction from the shopkeepers and business community of the Haute Ville. Morisset even quotes an antisemitic article, from a 1900 edition of *La Semaine Commerciale*, describing Saint Roch as 'le repaire des petits marchands juifs' (Morisset, 1999, p. 134). During the 20th century, the predominant image of Saint Roch was that of a transit zone, through which one either passed socially (on the way, conceivably, to life in the Haute Ville), or physically (to help create direct links between the Haute Ville and the *banlieue*, part of the district was destroyed to make way for a motorway terminating on the parliament hill, which takes the civil servants of the Quiet Revolution to their offices). The motorway pillars are the site of a very active graffiti culture. Today, the district's future seems bound up with a revalorisation of its history and its 'underground' vocation.

If the meanings and representations circulating around Québec City are deeply structured by its topographies of hierarchy, these still cannot provide a full understanding about the content of those structures: the realities of working-class life, the relationships between narratives of class, ethnicity and nationhood, or the question of change, as in the fact of the francophone reconquest of the city, and of economic and demographic ups and downs. The question of who are or were the Québecquois (to differentiate them from the 'Québécois' inhabiting the province as a whole) is perhaps best explained by the city's distinctness vis-à-vis its great rival, Montréal.

Not Montréal

By 1830, Québec City had been overtaken in population by Montréal (and by Toronto in 1870). By 1901, Montréal was five times more populous. Québec City's relative peripheralisation in terms of the new industrial economies of both Québec as a whole and of Canada was due to several factors. Firstly, the progressive dredging of the St Lawrence permitted ocean-going ships to sail upstream as far as Montréal. Opposed as early as 1824 by Québec City when it was first mooted by Montréal businessmen, the process was virtually complete by the early 1860s. In 1853, Québec City exported 62 per cent of Canada's products, compared to Montréal's 19 per cent, but in 1861 these figures had reversed. The decline in timber exports provoked, amongst other reasons, by the rise of the metal-hulled ship — which in turn affected the city's shipbuilding industry — was also a contributing factor. In addition, Québec City was late in connecting to Canada's railway network, the link with Montréal completed only in 1879. A southern branch had earlier favoured Lévis and the south shore, but the railway bridge over the St Lawrence was not completed until 1917.

Economic stagnation — despite the advantages afforded by being made the provincial capital at Confederation in 1867 — also explains the decline in the anglophone population, from 40 per cent of the total in 1860 to 16 per cent in 1901. Another factor in this development was the withdrawal of the British garrison in 1871. Those anglophones had included a large proportion of Irish, of course, as in the first half of the 19th century Québec City had been the main arrival port for immigrants to Canada. In 1832, 60,000 such immigrants passed through the city and, between 1829 and 1865, one million in total did so. Forming 28 per cent of the population in 1861, the Irish composed 60 per cent of all immigrants in the 1830s and 90 per cent in the 1840s. To an extent, hierarchies and differentiations between Catholic and Protestant Irish were reproduced in the city, with many of the latter being skilled shipbuilding labourers and the former predominantly hired daily for work in the docks. As a result, around a quarter of the Protestant Irish lived in the Haute Ville and only 10 per cent of the Catholics. The insalubrious rue Champlain, in a narrow part of the Basse Ville between the cliff face and the river, was home, along with the rue Saint-Pierre, to over half of the Catholics. Rivalries between Irish and French-Canadian dockworkers led to street confrontations in 1866–7 (see Courville & Gardon, 2001, pp. 207–9). Relations between the two communities were thus extremely complex, as they often shared both religious affiliation and economic status. Rivals in the latter domain, they were also divided on linguistic grounds, but suspicion of the Irish by the clergy's conservative element, as representing the threat of anglicisation, was not necessarily borne out by the experience of mixed marriages, within which the Irish were often assimilated into the French language.

Québec City's economic decline in the late 19th century, in relation to Montréal, was relative and in fact represented a *francisation* that in some ways prefigured aspects of the Quiet Revolution of the 1960s. Only with the language laws passed by the Parti Québécois in 1977 can a linguistic — if not ethnic — 'reconquest' of Montréal be described (Levine, 1990), but the francophone face of Québec City had been re-established long before. This was due in part to a rural exodus[5] (a third of the city's 1901 population had been born in the countryside) impelled by the massive birth rate of the 19th century — the famous *revanche des berceaux*, which had ensured the survival of a French-speaking people in this part of North America. Also significant, was the emerging francophone business class which set this cheap labour to work in labour-intensive industries such as shoe, corset and furniture manufacture and took advantage of the spaces left by the largely Anglo-owned timber and shipbuilding enterprises, whose owners relocated elsewhere or transferred into the financial sector. One of Canada's major 20th-century confrontations on ethnic and linguistic lines was thus played out in Québec City in 1918, when riots over conscription led to four civilians being shot dead by the Canadian

5   To an extent, this process is being repeated in the early 21st century, as Québec's regions empty.

army. However, the ethnic hearth of the French-Canadians was also profoundly divided on class lines. By 1901, the working-class districts of Saint-Sauveur and Saint-Roch contained 60 per cent of the city's population. The bourgeoisie and *notables* of the Haute Ville still of course ran Québec on the traditional top down basis, but were more parochial and regional in their outlook than their Montréal equivalents.

It is clear then that, in contrast to Montréal, questions of topography and power, homogenisation and peripheralisation, in Québec City, interlink in turn with those of port and fortress, *ouverture* and *chambranle*. Moreover, the latter structuring needs to be expressed diachronically, via gerunds which express a *rhythm* of opening and closing according to circumstances. Nowhere is this better expressed than in the relations between heritage (memory and identity) and tourism (the world as it invests Québec City) which so dominate its physical space today.

Heritage and Tourism

The beginning of the Quiet Revolution coincided with the emergence of innovative *cinéma direct* documentaries from the National Film Board of Canada (NFB), and with them what might properly be called a Québec national cinema. *Québec-USA ou l'invasion pacifique*, the short documentary made in 1962 by Michel Brault and Claude Jutra, neatly summarises certain tensions in Québec City's identity as a tourist destination. While poking gentle fun at American visitors to Québec City, it expresses in minor mode a nationalist discourse that even in the 1960s established homologies between the situation in Québec and movements in the Third World. In combination with images of Catholic schools teaching French as a second language and of a visiting American destroyer, a guided *promenade* by a middle-class African-American couple both continues techniques that emphasise the jarring contrast between cultures (large American car in narrow streets, swing music contrasting with traditional Québec fiddles on the soundtrack) and raises questions for the Québec audience.

The *promenade* includes a visit to the Plains of Abraham: the tourists' confusion (they are uncertain as to whether an equivalent of the Louisiana Purchase was enacted here) only serves to underline the meaning of this place for a Québec audience. As the car enters the precincts of the parliament building, the motto of Québec — 'Je me souviens' — is spelled out in a flower arrangement. For if memory itself has a history, what meanings attach to it when it is expressed as an admonition, in a context that is one of national reassertion and is overdetermined by its relationship with its giant neighbour to the south? And how does the motto relate to the numerous 'souvenir' shops that, glimpsed from a car window, are seen to line the highway from the frontier as it approaches the city? A reflex answer would be to posit a binary opposition between the authenticity of Québec's national identity and its commodification in tourist form.

Québec-USA ou l'invasion pacifique entertains that notion but, more interestingly, makes it coexist ambiguously with the attractions of North American and indeed European modernity (an anti-manicheanism which may partly explain the choice of an African-American couple. Thus the final sequence and closing credits feature the terrasse Dufferin as a space of freedom, social mixing, *flânerie* and sexual flirtation, the equivalent of a boulevard which drowns the memory of a clerical past represented by the occasional nun. Visually, this short film encapsulates the dual nature of those Québec films that contain a transnational element, that is recognition of 'us' and 'our' cityscapes and landscapes and also a look at 'us' as perceived by others.

A recent work comparing the cultural geographies of Québec City and New Orleans confirms this constant interaction, the potential destabilisations of which I would seek to emphasise:

> Ainsi, si les lieux de mémoire sont les réceptacles des symboles culturels
> partagés par une population locale homogène, ils n'en demeurent
> pas moins des centres appropriés par le regard de l'Autre, le visiteur,
> à la recherche d'une ambiance culturelle authentique dans un but de
> divertissement et d'évasion. L'identité collective ne choisit-elle pas
> d'être confirmée par le touriste pour des raisons d'ordre idéologique ou
> économique? Les transformations dans la ville, dues à cette interaction
> entre le dedans et le dehors, l'homogène et l'hétérogène, le mondial et le
> local, doivent être décodées par les géographes. (Geronimi, 2003, p. 25)

This can also be read as the tension between Québec City as 'home' (founding *foyer* of the Québec nation and of the French-Canadian people), and as heterotopia (tourist, but not exclusively so), entered via a rigmarole (here, the opening sequence at the frontier and the emphasis on crossing the bridge).

As we have seen, Québec City's tourist and heritage vocation has a history, with different determinants that can be traced diachronically, and this in turn means that struggles for meaning have circulated around it. As we noted earlier, 18th-century British notions of the picturesque played a key role in the 'envisioning' of Québec City in the period after the Conquest. This had emerged out of the aesthetics of landscape painting, such as that of Claude Lorrain, and took the form of an idealising, dehistoricising and depoliticising gaze, somewhere between contemporary notions of the beautiful and the sublime, which produced ways of viewing the 'new imperial spaces' (Crowley, 2005, p. 25; see, for example, Andrews, 1989). Indeed, a novel, *The History of Emily Montague* (1768), by Frances Brooke, wife of an army chaplain in Québec, also played its part in this cultural development.

Martine Geronimi traces this Romantic discourse in British guide books of the 1820s and 1830s, and how, as the century progressed, the city became a destination of choice, particularly for American visitors. They possessed a certain cultural capital and were attracted not only by Québec City's scenic aspects, appreciation of which was magnified by the increased industrialisation of western society, but also the connotations of history and of an exotic 'Frenchness' (Geronimi, 2003, pp. 95–7). Only with the spread of motor car ownership in the US from the second decade of the next century onwards, were these visitors supplanted by newer middle-class tourists. Lord Dufferin himself embodied the penetration of elites with discourses about both 'heritage' and hygienism and efficiency. In a speech delivered in June 1876, he interpellated the City Council as 'trustees on behalf of civilizations and the inhabitants of the whole American continent — by whom the ruin and degradation of its antique battlements would be regarded as an irreparable outrage and a common loss', while at the same time, in a gesture favouring spectacle and a new urbanism, foreseeing 'one continuous uninterrupted pathway for pedestrians' to produce 'a walk which for its convenience, freedom from noise, danger and interruption, for the variety and beauty of its points of view, and for its historical and civic interest, will be absolutely unequalled' (quoted in Geronimi, 2003, p. 127). Indeed, the pragmatics of seeking a tourist market played a major role in this period of decline in the city's traditional activities.

The first guide in French to Québec City did not appear until 1880. Official contacts between France and Québec had been limited since the Conquest and the French Revolution, but were reinaugurated with the visit of the warship *La Capricieuse* in 1855, which coincided with ceremonies commemorating the war dead of 1759, some of whose bones had been discovered in 1852. Anniversaries such as the tercentenary of 1908 and 'the 400th' of 2008 celebrated by this book played an important role in the imagined recreation of links. The dominant discourse of heritage in Québec City since 1960 has been that of the Quiet Revolution, which set out to complete the symbolic re-appropriation of the city — now unambiguously understood to be a *national* capital — by its francophone inhabitants:

> Le Vieux-Québec devait être la pierre angulaire de la promotion de
> cette nouvelle vision d'une identité distincte, en tant que fait historique
> <<concret>>. Le Vieux-Québec (…) s'imposait comme le lieu devant
> être restauré, re-fabriqué, et re-francisé pour devenir symboliquement le
> <<berceau>> de l'Amérique française.(Courville & Garon, 2001, p. 273;
> see also Geronimi, 2003, pp. 163–9)

As Marc Saint-Hilaire points out, the decision in the 1960s to restore the 17th-century architecture of the Place Royale in the Vieux Port represented a move away from both clerical and anglophone investments. This urban square, not the nearby rural Ile d'Orléans, was to be seen as the cradle of French Canada, a space distinct from the seminary and Ursulines convent, from the citadel associated with the British military past and from the Château Frontenac in the Haute Ville. A long battle had been waged during the 20th century to conserve the architectural heritage of the city in the face of modernisation such as that embodied by construction of the 17-storey Price Building of 1929. This began with the creation of a Commission d'Urbanisme et de Conservation in 1928 and culminated in 1963 with the Loi sur les Monuments Historiques declaring the old city to be an *arrondissement historique*, with wide powers of protection given to the City Council. In 1985, Québec City's World Heritage status was recognised by UNESCO.

This 'refabrication' of the city extends to the numerous *lieux de mémoire*, indeed a politics of commemoration is actively pursued by the Commission de la capitale nationale du Québec, established in 1995. Since that date there has been a spate of new plaques and statues. The *promenade* envisaged and created by Lord Dufferin was also of course a walk through memory, but an ill-defined and vague Walter Scott-type memory of medieval, pre-industrial Europe. A promenade through contemporary Québec City reveals a site saturated with signs and symbols, a veritable *mise en scène* and spectacularisation of heritage. An exhaustive list and an analysis are provided in Courville and Garon's work (2001, pp. 388–403). The National Assembly's façade consists of 22 statues and two allegorical groupings, which form a microcosm of the repartition of categories elsewhere in the city: predominance of the New France period over that of British rule and of politicians, explorers, religious figures and the military.

Robert Lepage

Québec City's relative linguistic homogeneity and foundational status do not in any sense mean that it is a unified space. But the comparison with Montréal raises the question of what contestations — and what cultural production — might arise in relation to the *outside* and to the world beyond, in addition to those *internal* differences, and the obvious example of tourism, that we have examined. It is the theatre and film director Robert Lepage who has most famously portrayed the surprising and particular global irruptions that manifest themselves in the seemingly enclosed spaces of Québec City and that are so different from the everyday negotiations of the flows of Montréal. Born in Québec City in 1957 to a working-class family that included adopted anglophone siblings, Lepage has pursued his theatre career either there (his collaborative troupe, Ex Machina, has been based in a converted fire station in the rue Dalhousie in the Vieux Port since 1997) or abroad, thus leapfrogging over Montréal.[6]

A scene in Lepage's second feature film, *Le Polygraphe* (1996, set in 1989), encapsulates his procedure. Doctoral student François (Patrick Goyette) is accompanying his neighbour Lucie (Marie Brassard) and her new lover Christof (Peter Stormare) along the walls of Québec City. They are returning from the Château Frontenac where he works as a waiter. All three are linked in a narrative that is a variation on Québec noir, as François is suspected — wrongly, as it turns out — of the murder of his girlfriend, Lucie is to play the role of the latter in a film and Christof is a police pathologist and friend of François's interrogator. François and Christof are also linked thematically, in that Christof is an East German refugee and François's thesis is about political exile. The walls in these shots therefore have multiple connotations, but first and foremost they represent the massive weight and presence of the past, a frequent theme in Lepage's work. A parallel is also created when Christof traverses the Berlin Wall.

Since Montréal lends itself much more to such an image of Manichean division (as in Jean Forest's *Le Mur de Berlin P.Q.* of 1983), other readings are entirely possible. As François takes his leave, a high-angle shot reverse shot frames him against the walls, while the others are photographed from a low angle with nothing else in the frame but the night sky and swirling snow particles. A vast contrast of contraction and dilation is caught here: the walled old town and the cosmos. But there is also an interchangeability and an implied movement between them: the infinite sky is also the domain of minute particles; the wall is the repository of the vast archive of the past. In addition, the relativisation of truth that takes place in the film, via the uncertain lie-detector test, and especially the motif of the *matrushka* dolls, suggests that the walls of old Québec City are but one membrane in a perhaps endless series of interconnecting cells, a variation on the concentricity that characterises the spaces of Québec City.

Already by 1985, Lepage's epic theatre production *The Dragon's Trilogy* had been staged, which traced its characters from the city's old Chinatown in the 1930s — since demolished — across the whole world. Lepage's first feature film, *Le Confessionnal* (1995), contains many examples of contraction and dilation, of the juxtaposition of a tiny point and of a universe beyond, which are harnessed to a geography and history of Québec City, with implications for Québec as a whole and for the wider world. In its closing scene, Pierre

6 See, for example, his evocation of the enrichment provided and 'horizons' opened up by his work with Peter Brook, Peter Gabriel, the National Theatre in London and Dramaten in Stockholm and their relationship with the 'petit centre' at Québec City and his work which remains 'profondément québecois' (Charest, 1995, p. 56).

Lamontagne (Lothaire Bluteau) is carrying a child on his shoulders as they walk precariously along the parapet of the Pont de Québec, the steel girder bridge across the St Lawrence in Québec City. The child is the product of the liaison of his adoptive brother Marc (Patrick Goyette), a rent-boy, and a striptease artist, Manon (Anne-Marie Cadieux) and is the third generation of a family afflicted by diabetes. It is the realisation of the hereditary nature of this disease that has revealed the central enigma of the film, the identity of Marc's father. His mother Rachel (Suzanne Clément), after giving birth in 1953 to this illegitimate child at the age of 16, then committed suicide by throwing herself off the same bridge. In the film's two time frames of 1952 and 1989, suspicion had fallen on the priest, Massicotte (Normand Daneau), who had then lost his position, but by 1989 he had become a diplomat/politician (Jean-Louis Millette) and the lover/client of Marc. True paternity lay with Pierre's recently deceased father Paul-Emile Lamontagne (François Papineau), who had had sex with Rachel while she lived in the family home they shared with his wife and her sister Françoise (Marie Gignac).

This narrative is overlaid with references to, and extracts from, Hitchcock's *I Confess* (1952), in which a murderer confesses his crime to a Catholic priest (Montgomery Clift), who then falls under suspicion himself because the murder victim was blackmailing him, but he is unable to reveal the truth to the police due to the seal of confessional. The opening montage of *I Confess* cuts from various locations in the city, eventually homing in on the murder scene: these include the Château Frontenac, shot from a low angle on the river, but in silhouette, and then from an extremely low and distorted angle. The gothic, hierarchical and labyrinthine nature of the city is emphasised by the expressionist, high-contrast black and white photography and effectively inaugurates *Québec noir*. This film is an adaptation of a 1902 French play, *Nos Deux Consciences*, by Paul Anthelme. As Martin Lefebvre has pointed out, any other urban setting would probably have necessitated a period or costume film treatment of the story (Lefebvre, 1998, pp. 88–98).[7]

The year 1952, as Pierre's opening voiceover makes clear, is also significant for having seen the advent of television in Québec and the electoral victory of the clerical-nationalist politician, Maurice Duplessis. *Le Confessionnal* contrasts the priest-ridden society of traditional Québec with the decidedly post-traditional late 1980s, in which the production of subjectivity that takes place in the confessional box has shifted to the grids, lattices and booths associated with a gay sauna and the suburban strip club. It also abounds with references to

---

7   In fact, the film was one of several Hollywood productions made in Canada in the period, following an agreement between the Canadian government and the majors, one aim of which was to promote tourism in Canada.

other films by Hitchcock, who is seen as bringing Hollywood — and therefore the world — to Québec City. As the film moves back and forth from 1952 to 1989, it sets up tiny circuits of contrast, but also exchange, between the local and the global and between past and present. These include: womb and cinema screen (and beyond it Hollywood and the world), as Pierre's mother attends the premiere of *I Confess*, an event narrated in voiceover by the adult Pierre; the hand gesture of two (horizontal) fingers designating 'very little' made by the verger when asked by Hitchcock's assistant (Kristin Scott Thomas) whether he speaks English; and the astonishing cut from Renée Hudon, a little girl auditioning for Hitchcock, who reads news from 1989 about Tiananmen Square from a script, to a television image of the adult Renée Hudon reading the news on Québec City's SRC channel (a cross-reference only fully understood by a local TV audience). In addition, editing cuts, and even movement within the same shot, serve to make frequent connections between the two time periods, even to the point of rendering them — momentarily at least — indiscernible. For example, the camera tracks from right to left in the early scene of the father's funeral in 1989, along the (empty) church to reach the (packed) congregation of 1952, or from the mother's miscarriage in the bathroom in 1952 to Pierre reorganising the flat in 1989.

This rhythm of contraction and dilation features throughout the film as it spans the local (indeed, the very local, even the quasi-incestuous; witness the scenes in the 1952 Lamontagne household, especially the kitchen) and the global (Pierre has just returned from studying in China, Marc accompanies Massicotte to Japan and commits suicide there). These features and the playing with time are consistent with Deleuzean film theory. Deleuze develops out of Bergson the notion of the virtual shadowing the actual, a concept based on the idea of time consisting of 'presents that pass' and 'a past that is conserved': the virtual image is 'l'actuel présent *dont* elle est le passé, absolument et simultanément', and in cinema this can give rise to what he calls the 'crystal-image' (Deleuze, 1985, pp. 106–7):

> Contracter l'image, au lieu de la dilater. Chercher le plus petit circuit
> qui fonctionne comme limite intérieure de tous les autres (...) ce point
> d'indiscernibilité, c'est précisément le plus petit cercle qui le constitue,
> c'est-à-dire la coalescence de l'image actuelle et de l'image virtuelle, l'image
> biface, actuelle et virtuelle à la fois. (Deleuze, 1985, pp. 92–3)

Le Confessionnal thus addresses in an original way the relations between Québec City and the world. There remains to be examined the significance of the last scene and the final city site represented, namely the Pont de Québec. This is, after all, the site 'where the river narrows', the first settlement which 300 years later gave rise to this first bridge. Next to it is a road-only bridge, the Pont Pierre-Laporte, built in 1970 and named after a government minister murdered by the Front de Libération du Québec, another example of a foundational dimension of meaning in the precincts of Québec City.[8]

The ambiguous ending of *Le Confessionnal*, in contrast, shows how 'we' are contemporaneous with the child, just as Québec is swollen with its past. Pierre and the child not only form a vertical line perched on the bridge and over the flowing but unseen river, punctuating the passage of the present, they also form one continuous human figure, adult and child, 'le passé porte le présent comme un enfant sur ses épaules', and why not the reverse, the present carrying the past on its shoulders, the past of the adult as child? All these possibilities form a potentially new conception of nation-time, which enables a revitalisation and problematisation of 'our' perception of the present, reinstating the child, making visible the historical sedimentation, emphasising connectedness. Both Deleuze and Lepage use the word 'tectonic' to describe this kind of image and artistic practice (Deleuze, 1985, pp. 317, 321).[9]

As Deleuze puts it, 'les personnes et les choses occupent dans le temps une place incommensurable à celle qu'ils tiennent dans l'espace' (Deleuze, 1985, p. 56). The bridge is also a bridge of ghosts: in 1907, 75 workers were killed on it as the nearly complete south cantilever arm crashed into the river and in 1916, 13 men died as the central span fell into the St Lawrence as it was being manoeuvred into position.[10] But the ambiguity of Pierre and the child's tightrope walk is that it is also about the future, an uncertain and therefore open future that takes them out of the city. Of course the main place outside the city limits that has been represented in the film is the suburb of Charny, notably the strip club and motel where Manon lives with the child and an Amerindian, Moose (Billy Merasty), with whom she performs her stage act. As Bruno Cornellier has argued (Cornellier, 2005–6, p. 61), this latter character has been neglected in analyses of the film, including my own. Anglophone with seemingly no knowledge of French, he embodies certain clichés of the representation of Amerindians in Canadian and the wider North American culture: the dancing Indian, eroticised and put into spectacle, presenting a non-threatening sexuality (unlike that of African-American men) now that the native population has safely undergone its historical defeat. In addition, he serves as a go-between, passing Marc's leather jacket to Pierre's ownership;

8   For a further discussion of the October Crisis and the 'foundational fictions' of Québec, see Marshall, 2001, pp. 37–45. This text also contains a fuller Deleuzean analysis of *Le Confessionnal*, pp. 305–12.

9   See also Lepage's play *Tectonic Plates* (adapted for television in Britain in 1993, directed by Peter Mettler).

10   For more on the significance of the Pont de Québec for Canadian culture, see Clandfield, 2003, pp. 2–15. Many of the dead workers were Mohawks from the reservation at Kahnawake near Montréal.

Pierre wears it in the final scenes with Massicotte, has grown his hair so that it is long and black like Moose's and he seems to have moved away from the passive and bewildered version of masculinity he embodies earlier in the film, resembling somewhat more the animal, *sauvage*-like sexuality represented by Marc:

> ces identités marginales se rejoignent et, projetées sur le corps neutre de Pierre, s'associent dans le fantasme au corps virtuel, <<mineur>>, nomade et polymorphe de l'Indien, *en transit* entre deux rives. (Cornellier, 2005–6, p. 61)

It is fitting to end this analysis of Québec City with the final scene of *Le Confessionnal*, for this film eloquently summarises the various tendencies to be found in representations of this French Atlantic space: those of *Québec noir* (all the street scenes away from the family home are filmed at night, for example), of populism and of the symbolic weight carried by the city. *Le Confessionnal*, as it hints at a Québec — and a Québec City — yet to come, plays on a tension between destiny and choice, past sediments and an open future.

REFERENCES

Andrews, Malcolm (1989) *The Search for the Picturesque: Landscape Aesthetics and Tourism in Britain, 1760–1800* (Chicago: Stanford University Press).

Bird, I. Lucy (1966) *The Englishwoman in North America* (Toronto University Press). Written 1856.

Blanchard, Raoul (1935) *L'Est du Canada français "Province de Québec", II.* Publications de l'Institut Scientifique Franco-Canadien (Paris: Masson).

Charest, Rémy, (1995) *Robert Lepage: Quelques zones de liberté* (Québec City: L'instant même/Ex Machina).

Clandfield, Peter, (2003) 'Bridgespotting: Lepage, Hitchcock and Landmarks in Canadian Film', *Canadian Journal of Film Studies*, 12, no. 1 (Spring), pp. 2–15.

Courville, Serge and Robert Garon (eds.) (2001) *Québec: ville et capitale* (Québec City: Sainte-Foy, Laval).

Cornellier, Bruno, (2005–6) 'L'Indien, mon frère: identité, nationalité et indianité dans *Le Confessionnal*', *London Journal of Canadian Studies*, 21, pp. 49–70.

Crowley, John E. (2005) '"Taken on the Spot": The Visual Appropriation of New France for the Global British Landscape', *Canadian Historical Review*, 86, no. 1 (March), pp. 1–28.

Deleuze, Gilles (1985) *L'Image-Temps* (Paris: Minuit).

Geronimi, Martine (2003) *Québec et la Nouvelle-Orléans: paysages imaginaires français en Amérique du nord* (Paris: Belin).

Grignon, Marc (1997) *"Loing du soleil": Architectural Practice in Quebec City during the French Regime* (New York: Peter Lang).

Grignon, Marc (1999) 'Comment s'est faite l'image d'une ville: Québec du XVIIe au XIXe siécle', in Lucie K. Morisset and Denis Saint-Jacques (eds.), *Ville imaginaire, ville identitaire: échos de Québec* (Québec: Nota bene), pp. 99–117.

Hare, John, Marc Lafrance and David-Thiery Ruddel (1987) *Histoire de la ville de Québec 1608–1871* (Montréal: Boréal/Musée canadien des civilisations), p. 306.

Lapierre, Laurier L. (1992) *1759 Battle for Canada* (Toronto: McClelland & Stewart).

Lefebvre, Martin (1998) 'A Sense of Time and Place: the Chronotope in *I Confess* and *Le Confessionnal*', *Québec Studies*, 26 (Fall/Winter), pp. 88–98.

Létourneau, Jocelyn (2006) *Que veulent vraiment les Québécois? Regard sur l'intention nationale au Québec (français) d'hier à aujourd'hui* (Montréal: Boréal).

Levine, Marc V. (1990) *The Reconquest of Montreal: Language Policy and Social Change in a Bilingual City* (Philadelphia: Temple University Press).

Marshall, Bill (2001) *Quebec National Cinema* (Montreal: McGill-Queen's University Press), pp. 37–45.

Morisset, Lucie K., and Luc Noppen (eds), *Patrimoine du quartier Saint-Roch* (Québec City: Ville de Québec, Division du design urbain et du patrimoine, 1995).

Morisset, Lucie K. (1999) 'Créer l'identité par l'image: sémiogenèse de la *ville basse* de Québec', in Lucie K. Morisset, Luc Noppen and Denis Saint-Jacques (eds.), *Ville imaginaire, ville identitaire: échos de Québec* (Québec: Nota bene), pp. 119–40.

Parent, Alain (2005) *Entre Empire et Nation: les représentations de la ville de Québec et de ses environs, 1760–1833* (Sainte-Foy: Presses de l'Université Laval).

Pratt, Mary Louis (1992) *Imperial Eyes: Travel Writing and Transculturation* (London: Routledge).

4

FORGETTING FRANCE OR FORGING A NEW NATION: A STAGE IN *CANADIEN* WRITING (1825–45)

Éric Wauters

Each month between September 1827 and February 1828, an extract from Louis-François Raban's *Petite biographie des Députés de France* (Raban, 1826) appeared in a new journal, *Bibliothèque canadienne*, founded and edited by Michel Bibaud (Bibaud, 1827–8). These six satirical biographies about members of the legislative Chamber in France were often amusing, to judge by this entry: 'Lebeschu de Champsavin, aged 70, height: 5 feet 6 inches, hair: none, legislative influence: none'; and this on Peyronnet, who 'was so eloquent that he never spoke on the floor without causing the whole assembly to burst out laughing; even the silent ones had to bite their lips to stop themselves chuckling.'[1] The book also contained several entries about deputies snoozing on the job and obsequious government bootlickers.

The majority of individuals depicted (and often caricatured) in this lengthy lampoon were probably unknown to most Canadians and the biographical and political allusions would have been difficult to grasp except by a tiny minority au fait with current affairs in France. How then can we explain the amount of space devoted to France in a publication aimed at a limited readership of affluent subscription-paying Canadian readers?[2]

I

The emphasis given to this satirical examination of the *Députés de France* is in fact quite remarkable in view of the limited attention Bibaud's magazine generally accorded to news from France.[3] In addition to anecdotes and witticisms (not

---

1   'Peyronnet: son éloquence est d'une telle nature qu'il n'est jamais monté à la tribune sans être aussitôt accueilli par les éclats de rire de l'assemblée; les muets eux-mêmes sont forcés de se mordre les lèvres pour ne pas éclater'.

2   The word 'Canadian' is used here with its 19th-century meaning: a French-speaking British subject in North America.

3   Biographies (at times critical) about Bibaud, the main protagonist of this chapter, have been

all by French authors), it would sometimes feature unusual facts, such as an extraordinarily huge oak in the Vosges Mountains.[4] Thereafter, perhaps due to a lack of resources, the magazine focused more on Canadian affairs. It may also have been because the one-time mother country had changed too much in the aftermath of the cataclysmic French Revolution. The Canadian texts of the past 30 years had been uniformly negative about this fateful event for its 'unbelievable cruelties' against the king and religion. One such diatribe from 1799 went as follows:

> Chantons de Nelson le courage,
> Couronnons son front de lauriers;
> Des Français, il dompte la rage;
> Rien ne résiste à nos guerriers.
> Conservons notre monarchie,
> Respectons le trône des rois ;
> Détestons l'affreuse anarchie,
> Qui réduit la France aux abois. (Huston (comp.), 1848–50)

We know that religious issues were particularly sensitive for Canadians. In 1820, Ludger Duvernay published a monthly religious newspaper, *L'Ami de la religion et du roi*, for which exiled French priests acted as zealous propagandists and Trois-Rivières priest, Louis-Marie Cadieux, was unofficial director. For some of Bibaud's friends, such as the physician and journalist, Jacques Labrie, or the first mayor of Montréal, Jacques Viger — both supporters of Ultramontanism (a Roman Catholic philosophy that asserts the superiority of Papal authority over secular national governments and local ecclesiastical hierarchies) — there would have been a crisis of conscience when forced to choose between the new socially evangelical doctrine and loyalty to Rome. Duvernay also published a fake Canadian version of *Paroles d'un croyant* by Catholic priest Felicité de Lamennais, an evangelical tract that could potentially have become one of the ideological foundations of the 'Patriotes'. However Pope Gregory XVI had condemned it and Jean-Jacques Lartigue, Auxiliary Bishop of Québec in Montréal, accordingly urged Canadians to remain loyal to ultramontane orthodoxy and abstain from politics.

Also significant was the pervading presence of 'l'usurpateur Bonaparte' in some Canadian reviews, not as a political hero but as a charismatic character:

---

written by Sicotte (1908), Malchelosse (1945) and Perrault (1951). Studies of his journalistic work include Bujila (1960) and Schonberger (1977). His political commitment is discussed by Frégault (1944–5) and Tousignant (1974). An excellent summary appears in Céline Cyr's *Dictionnaire biographique du Canada en ligne* (www.biographi.ca).

4   The *Variétés* book pages of July and August 1826 contained the only extensive news about French arts or literature, drawn mainly from Paris newspapers but with a sprinkling of comments from British press sources.

his biography, his personality, the man 'undressed and stripped of his coat',[5] were endlessly fascinating (as was also the case in Britain, a country hardly in favour of Bonapartism). An example that bears testimony to the revolutionary context of the times was an 1835 piece, 'Souvenir de Napoléon, couplets chantés au banquet de la Société Française en Canada, à Montréal, air: *De la Marseillaise*', which included the line: 'Be immortal, oh hero that we mourn!'.[6]

We might initially assume that Bibaud sought only to amuse his readers with the *Députés de France* series … or simply to beef up each issue. His review contains numerous anecdotes or witty epigrams (by Voltaire, Rivarol and so on) and we know that padding was a widespread practice in journalism. But this does not satisfactorily explain why the series continued for six months. Bibaud justified the prolonged run as follows:

> Nous aurions pu, en publiant ces extraits, les faire précéder d'un bout de *préface*, accompagnée d'une courte introduction, suivie elle-même d'un mot d'*avant-propos* ; mais tout cela est du vieux style, et nous n'en ferons rien. Nous aurions pu, de même, y joindre quelques commentaires, faire quelques parallèles, *pointer* certains rapprochements, &c. Nous n'en ferons rien encore; laissant à nos lecteurs tout le mérite et tout le plaisir des petites applications auxquelles ces extraits peuvent prêter.

In fact, mocking drowsy or subservient deputies is a universal practice in parliamentary regimes and with several of the entries it was easy to make amusing parallels with certain prominent Canadians:

> Poydavant. Il dort pendant le temps des séances, vote en bâillant et ne se réveille que pour demander la clôture.

> Nicolaï […] c'est un lion avec ses administrés et un agneau avec les ministres. A la tribune, ce n'est pas un aigle.

> Colligny (de). Le résultat des démarches que nous avons faites pour savoir à quoi ce député employait le temps de la session, est que lorsqu'il ne mange pas, il dort, et lorsqu'il ne dort pas, il mange — chez les ministres bien entendu.

> Mieulle (de). C'est un petit homme qui a fait son petit chemin et qui, grâce à son petit savoir faire, possède une petite fortune de 2 millions. Il fait quelquefois de petits discours et propose de petits amendements; ce qui ne l'empêche pas d'être le petit serviteur des ministres.

---

5 'Déshabillé et dépouillé de son manteau' in *Mes souvenirs sur Napoléon, sa famille et sa cour, par Mᵐᵉ Vᵛᵉ du général Durand*, 'à vendre à Montréal, chez Fabre & Cie', extracts in *Bibliothèque canadienne* (Jan. and Feb. 1827).

6 'Sois immortel, héros que nous pleurons!', *Répertoire*, vol. I, 1848, p. 306.

It was not just the references to real people that were entertaining, but also the fact that the majority of entries lampooned deputies associated with the right, such as Jaquinot-Pampelune:

> On pourrait dire que M. Jaquinot est né procureur du roi; ennemi juré de la presse, il s'éleva constamment contre l'institution du jury et soutint que la police ne pouvait jamais avoir tort … C'est le plus terrible antagoniste des auteurs, éditeurs, imprimeurs et libraires. La vue d'un journal lui fait mal; et si l'on fait de l'esprit dans le département de la Seine, ce n'est pas sa faute.

Of the 200 *Petite Biographie* entries published by Bibaud, some 20 are serious rather than comic. These concern a 'few outstanding opposition members',[7] liberal deputies like Casimir Perrier, Benjamin Constant, Royer-Collard and so on, who 'never failed to defend people's or the nation's interests'. Devaux is depicted as 'un homme de bien; c'est un franc libéral, qui a souvent l'honneur d'être injurié par les journaux vendus au pouvoir'. Dupont, who would soon play an important part in the 1830 Revolution, 'aima mieux perdre sa place [he was deputy of Rouen] que de transiger avec sa conscience, alors que cette place était presque toute sa fortune'. Following re-election in Paris in 1824, he was lauded thus: 'il n'a pas cessé de défendre les intérêts de son pays contre les empiètements ministériels'. Homage was also paid to opposition leader, General Maximilien Foy, upon his death in 1825:

> La France en deuil pleure encore la perte de ce grand citoyen: cent mille Français suivirent ses dépouilles mortelles jusqu'à leur dernière demeure, et une souscription ouverte pour doter sa famille, s'éleva promptement à un million. Le cadre de cet ouvrage ne nous permet pas d'entrer dans de longs détails; mais quels sont les Français qui ne connaissent pas les belles actions de ce grand homme qui fut l'un des premiers capitaines de l'armée, l'appui de la liberté et le prince des orateurs.

Though well known in France, Foy's reputation meant little to Canadians. We can therefore assume that padding or the reporting of witty remarks were not the only reasons for publication of these extracts. For example, the old Marquis of Bouville is praised thus: 'Freedom and equality have not a more formidable adversary; every time there is an opportunity to fight these two children of the Revolution, this deputy enters the fray, despite his great age'. We can therefore suppose that entries were not randomly selected and that Bibaud's review could hardly be described as politically neutral. Bringing France to people's attention was surely intentional and coincided with a leaflet produced in 1828 in New York by the *Courier des États-Unis, Journal Français, Politique*

---

7   Art. 'Basterreche', *Bibliothèque canadienne*, p. 129, Sept. 1827.

et Littéraire indicating that 'l'article consacré à la France occupera une place importante; [on] mentionnera les actes de ses gouvernements, les discussions de ses chambres, les décisions de ses tribunaux, etc.' The explanation becomes clear: the publishers, in their own words, 'deeply and perpetually support civil and religious freedom'. Was France a model for 'religious freedom' any longer? After the Revolution, such an assertion was curious at the very least.

To clarify that strange paradox, let us flash-back to the time of the French Revolution. From 1788 to 1794, three-quarters of the issues covered by *Gazette de Montréal*, published by Fleury Mesplet, commented on French events and reforms. In content terms, this coverage added up to some 40 per cent of the newspaper (205 pages out of 508).[8] Writing in January 1794, one of the editors, Henry Mézière, commented:

> les papiers révolutionnaires nous parvenaient alors, plus d'une fois nous
> les arrosâmes de nos pleurs, plus d'une fois ils furent portés en triomphe
> dans des clubs et dans des sociétés particulières au sein desquelles nous
> chantions l'aurore de la Liberté, ses progrès et ses luttes contre les nuages
> épais de la superstition et de la tyrannie. (de Lagrave, 1994, p. 389)

Such sentiments reflected circumstances in Canada rather than in France — they indicate enthusiasm for supporting a Constitution for Canada among those who contested the Constitutional Act of 1791 and formed political clubs in preparation for the elections of 1792. Mesplet himself was a fervent opponent of feudalism in Canada and the power of the Catholic church and a passionate advocate of judicial reform. Samuel Neilson's *Gazette de Québec* published similarly radical texts, by the French Revolutionary leader Marat among others, and carried a special issue about the French Constitution (5 January 1792). In 1791, Mesplet printed a pamphlet with the significant title, *The Northern Bastille*, clearly showing that events in France echoed local political developments.

The restoration of France into Canadian political literature around 1827 paralleled a local conflict with Canadian government and its institutions (more in its timing than ideologically). During the period that Bibaud's publication was running the satires about French deputies, Ludger Duvernay's *La Minerve* gave equal emphasis to news from France — the issues of 19 and 26 March and 9 April, 1827, for example, focused on how new legislation threatened the freedom of the French press. And it carried long extracts from speeches by Casimir Périer and Benjamin Constant, laid out in a way that was clearly not impartial. Its account (on 21 February, 1828) of the Parisian riots of November

---

8   218 of the 290 preserved issues (17 are missing) reported on the Revolution, including 165
     front pages: c.f. de Lagrave (1994), p. 357. For discussion of how the French Revolution
     affected Canada, see also Simard (1991) and Galarneau (1970).

1827 replicated the text of the report that appeared in *Le Constitutionnel*, France's main liberal publication, and similarly blamed government provocation for causing them. When Duvernay wrote about the reform and suppression of the French National Guard and simultaneously published letters about the Canadian militia, he drew a suggestive parallel between the two countries. But he did not focus solely on France: his newspaper also highlighted the Greek revolt, troubles in Ireland and the consequences of the latter for Catholics in the UK. By the end of the 1820s, Duvernay and others were effectively chronicling a new Atlantic Revolution, but from Canada and with reference to Canada. Any mentions of France in this journalistic canon were purely anecdotal.

II

Talking about revolution did not necessarily equate to being radical. These writers belonged to an educated and bilingual Canadian middle class, which was experiencing its own contradictions of identity and had more than one battle to fight. Brought up on French culture as its reading matter indicates, that middle class was torn between the need to defend its linguistic heritage and its sense of cultural inferiority, compared to Europe or the Anglo-Saxon world, and led to increased efforts to raise the level of Canadians' aestheticism. An entry on Canada in an English almanac from 1821 reports:

> The different tribes of Indians, or original natives, in Canada, are almost
> innumerable; but they have been observed to decrease in population where
> the Europeans are most numerous, owing chiefly to their immoderate
> use of spirituous liquor. A remarkable earthquake happened here in
> 1663, which overwhelmed a chain of mountains above 300 miles long,
> and changed their immense tract into a plain. Canada was conquered by
> the English, in 1759, and confirmed to them by the French at the peace
> of 1763. Soon after the declaration of war, by the United States against
> Great Britain, in 1812, the American government thought to have availed
> themselves of the opportunity which then offered of reducing this country,
> during the employment of the greater part of the British army, in the war
> on the continent of Europe. To effect this, no exertions on their part was
> spared; and upwards of 30,000 men entered Canada at different points,
> but were obliged to retire with great loss and disgrace, notwithstanding
> the vast inferiority of numbers that were opposed to them. In 1791, this
> country was divided into two provinces, Upper and Lower Canada, of
> which York and Quebec are the chief towns. [9]

There is nothing here about French-speaking people apart from one brief mention of Québec City. The question of Canadian identity had become very

9   *A General Gazetteer or Compendious Geographical Dictionary*, 15th edn., London, 1821,
   'originally compiled by R. Brookes', 1st edn. 1761.

acute by the mid 1820s. At the end of 1825, when the patriotic newspaper, *Le Canadien*, went bankrupt and was put up for sale, the *Montreal Herald* published a provocative letter applauding the disappearance of this 'nest of crows'. Michel Bibaud's reaction appeared on the first page of the *Bibliothèque Canadienne* in June 1826:

> La *Bibliothèque Canadienne* n'est pas, à proprement parler, un journal politique; mais c'est bien autant à la littérature canadienne, qu'à une politique qui ne lui conviendrait pas, qu'en veut l'écrivain en question, puisqu'il applaudit à la chute de l'*Abeille Canadienne*, comme à celle de tous les autres journaux en langue française.

As we shall see, Bibaud was still giving coverage to the issue of 'La Langue française' 18 years later, in the first article of his *L'Encyclopédie canadienne, journal scientifique et littéraire* (1842).

Building a national identity based on language represented a huge challenge for a Canadian elite, itself shaped by a mixed cultural heritage, as is evident from book advertisements and inventories of private libraries made once their owners had died. As Réjean Lemoyne showed in his MA thesis, British publications and authors dominated the Canadian book market up to approximately 1820 (Lemoyne, 1981).[10] The preponderance of British authors is confirmed by death inventories: in 1820–9, 55 per cent of authors represented were English and 27 per cent French (Labonté, 1986).[11] These figures reflect the fact that this bourgeoisie needed to protect its own linguistic identity, but was also class conscious, feeling closer to the English-speaking educated elite than to the French-speaking lower class, 'inhabitants of French origin, especially from the countryside, who, generally, don't understand English'.[12] In his article of June 1826, Bibaud continued:

> Si un petit nombre de Canadiens pensaient comme cet Anti-Canadien [the writer of a letter to the *Montreal Herald*], un grand nombre d'Anglais

10 In his analysis of 1,194 advertisements from *Gazette de Québec* (1764–1839) and *Le Canadien* (1831–9), Lemoyne found that the number of advertisements placed by authors or publishers were equally French and English (24% and 25%) and that the former only started to build up after the decade 1820–9.

11 The most frequently cited authors were Johnson, Scott, Voltaire and Robertson, followed by Blackstone, Fénelon, Hume and Wesley. However, such inventories were often drawn up following the death of an owner at an advanced age after building a private library over several decades: a time lag is therefore inevitable.

12 *Encyclopédie Canadienne*, no. 1, March 1842, p. 2. In two works published in 1855, *Tableau historique* and *Les institutions de l'Histoire du Canada* (see Bibliography), François-Maximilien Bibaud (Michel's son) noticed many anglicisms in Perrault's and Garneau's works, but owing to filial loyalty he may not have been completely impartial.

pensent autrement, c'est-à-dire d'une manière libérale et éclairée; plusieurs,
et des plus respectables, à Québec, à Montréal et ailleurs, nous ont fait
l'honneur de souscrire à ce journal, et presque pas un d'eux n'a retiré sa
souscription.

And in early 1828, Xavier Tessier, formerly editor of *Journal de Médecine de
Québec*, who was now editor of New York's *Journal des Sciences Naturelles*,
produced a leaflet deploring:

Les écrits en langue anglaise sont devenus si nombreux sur notre continent
qu'on serait tenté de croire que cette langue doit être bientôt la langue
scientifique du nouveau monde, surtout quand on envisage l'influence
que les États-Unis exercent déjà sur l'Amérique entière; et quoique le
nombre de ces écrits l'emporte peut-être sur leur utilité, on ne peut nier
que la langue anglaise ne possède aujourd'hui des richesses immenses, qui
sont presque perdues pour la nôtre [...]. L'immense population française
disséminée sur tous les points de l'Amérique ne connaît des travaux
précieux de la France moderne que ce qui lui est transmis par une langue
étrangère.[13]

One wonders how many Canadian people, apart from an intellectual minority,
were interested in this question. For example:

Nous nous sommes souvent étonnés que les descendants d'une race
à imagination aussi vive que l'étaient, à n'en pas douter, les anciens
Normands, eussent si peu à montrer en fait de littérature. Le défaut
d'instruction dans la grande masse de la population ne suffit pas pour
rendre raison de ce fait, puisque ce n'est pas de cette classe généralement
que la littérature attend son soutien, mais du petit nombre des personnes
éclairées, et ces personnes se trouvent, pensons-nous, à Montréal et à
Québec, aussi bien qu'à New York et à Londres.[14]

In a May issue of *Bibliothèque*, Bibaud reproduced an article that had appeared

---

13 *Bibliothèque*, Feb. 1828. Summary: 'Writings in English are so numerous in North America
that we might expect English to become the language of scientists in the New World,
especially if we take into account the influence the United States has throughout the whole
of America [...] We only know those precious works from modern France that have been
translated into a foreign language [English]'.

14 *L'Encyclopédie Canadienne*, no. 2: newspaper excerpt (no reference). Summary: 'the lack
of education in the greater part of the Norman population cannot explain their lack of
reading matter, since appreciation of literature was usually reliant upon a small well-
educated minority believed to be based in Montréal and Québec City as well as New York
and London.' Note that comparison with the descendants of the 'Old Normans' was a
fashionable theme in France too.

in the newspaper *La Minerve* (23 April 1827) on the theme 'What is a Canadian?':

> Généalogiquement, ce sont ceux dont les ancêtres habitaient le pays avant 1759, et les lois, les usages, leur sont politiquement conservés par des traités et des actes solennels; politiquement, les Canadiens sont tous ceux qui font cause commune avec les habitants du pays, quelle que soit leur origine; ceux qui ne cherchent pas à détruire la religion; ceux qui ont un intérêt réel et permanent dans le pays; ceux en qui le nom de ce pays éveille le sentiment de la patrie; ceux pour qui l'expropriation du peuple, au moyen des intérêts commerciaux, serait un malheur; ceux enfin qui ne voient pas un droit au-dessus de toutes les lois, dans les traitants venus d'outre-mer depuis 1759. Ceux-là sont les vrais Canadiens et il y a dans le pays un grand nombre d'Anglais respectables, que le pays reconnaît, parce que leurs intérêts sont les mêmes que les siens. [...] Les Canadiens français ne tendent pas à un pouvoir exclusif; ils n'ont pas de haine nationale contre les Anglais; et dès qu'un habitant du pays montre qu'il en est vraiment citoyen, on ne fait plus de différence. Mais ceux qui ne regardent le Canada que comme un poste de traite exclusive, un lieu où l'on peut vivre à même les deniers publics, ou s'enrichir pour retourner vivre ailleurs; ceux qui spéculent sur les propriétés du pays, on ne peut raisonnablement les reconnaître pour citoyens d'un pays qu'ils ne reconnaissent pas pour le leur, et qu'ils abandonneront au besoin, en secouant la poussière de leurs pieds [...]

> Dans tous les documents du temps [d'avant la conquête], nous trouvons que les *Canadiens* et les *Français* n'étaient pas la même chose. C'est qu'alors comme aujourd'hui, il y avait dans la colonie des habitants fixes et attachés au sol, et d'autres qui n'y venaient que pour faire fortune. [15]

Putting its bilingualism aside, the petite bourgeoisie was attracted to the English-speaking elite because it felt politically closer to England than to a changed, post-Revolution France. Bibaud and his friend Labrie admired the British constitution they were attempting to publicise: from December 1826 to February 1827, Bibaud published an 'Esquisse de la constitution britannique',

---

15 *Bibliothèque*, May 1827, no. 5, p. 219 onwards. In short: 'the Canadian is not just an inhabitant whose family has lived in the country since before 1759, nor just a French-speaking person. A Canadian is anyone who lives, works, contributes, abides by the laws and respects and loves the country. However, anyone who wants to take selfish advantage of Canadian society — by making money and leaving, for example — and has no long-term view, cannot be considered a true Canadian. This is what differentiates the true Canadian from the "colonial" French'.

with 'some reflections' and an 'author's response'. Also in 1827, Labrie published *Les premiers rudimens de la constitution britannique* [*Beginnings of the British Constitution*], 'with a historical summary and observations about the faults of the Canadian constitution and how to correct them, a useful work for everyone but especially Canadian youth'.[16] That same year, on 27 December, he gave a famous speech in Vaudreuil, reported in *La Minerve* on 7 January 1828, setting out his beliefs in British institutions and the constitution of Lower Canada, which had been led astray by the governor of Canada, Dalhousie, and his cronies in the legislative council. Bibaud was more reserved on this point as his journal's coverage of the debate reveals. But, as a historian, Bibaud was sympathetic to the colonial government and somewhat critical of the French Canadians and the Parti Canadien. Another friend, Viger, was not so favourably disposed towards British authority, but he revered the memory of the battle of Châteauguay,[17] and in1816 visited the battlefield with his friend Joseph Mermet, a royalist French officer in the British army. Later, he wrote 'Ma saberdache' [large wallet attached to a knight's belt], a long text with many references to the 1812 war, which Bibaud published.[18] As Fernand Ouellet rightly emphasised, commemoration of military events like these expressed the loyalty of French Canadians to Great Britain in the early 19th century (Ouellet, 1966 and 1976).[19] In 1831, for example, the *Répertoire national* included a piece entitled 'Le Voltigeur. Souvenirs de Chateauguay' (Huston, 1848, p. 185). On the one hand, it is true that Viger was politically sympathetic to Papineau, as his correspondence showed but, on the other, he and most Montrealers did not play an active part in the Patriot rebellion and Papineau accused him of 'modérantisme'. In 1848, the *Répertoire national* featured a 'Hymne Nationale' (sic), by Isidore Bédard, a deputy in the County of Saguenay. The ambiguity of this poem, dated 1829, was quite significant:

> Sol canadien, terre chérie!
> Par des braves tu fus peuplé;
> Ils cherchaient loin de leur patrie,
> Une terre de liberté. [...]
> Respecte la main protectrice

16 Translated from Brooke's essay, and 'précédés d'un précis historique, et suivis d'observations sur la constitution du Bas-Canada, pour en donner l'histoire et en indiquer les principaux vices, avec un aperçu de quelques-uns des moyens probables d'y remédier; ouvrage utile à toutes sortes de personnes et principalement destiné à l'instruction politique de la jeunesse canadienne', 1827.

17 The Canadian light infantrymen (*voltigeurs*) prevented an invasion by the US army.

18 *Bibliothèque*, Oct.–Dec. 1826, then March–Apr. 1827.

19 These have been translated and adapted by Claxton (1980).

D'Albion, ton digne soutien;
Mais fais échouer la malice
D'ennemis dans ton sein. […]
Si d'Albion la main chérie
Cesse un jour de te protéger,
Soutiens-toi seule, o ma patrie !
Méprise un secours étranger.
Nos pères sortis de la France
Étaient l'élite des guerriers,
Et leurs enfants de leur vaillance
Ne flétriront pas les lauriers.

How then do we escape from this mass of contradictions? It fell to writers to find three solutions to the problem of how to find a cultural identity.

III

The first solution was to put great effort into improving the cultural level of their compatriots, a purpose more easily achieved because these writers were also journalists. As far back as 1806, Jacques Labrie, then a medical student, was also the first editor of the biweekly *Courier de Québec*, founded by Pierre-Amable De Bonne, in which he featured political, literary, local and foreign news, as well as the newspaper's own research on the history of Canada. Bibaud published and wrote for many newspapers. In July 1817, he became editor of *L'Aurore*, a political, scientific and literary weekly which merged with *Le Spectateur canadien* in 1819, and from the following October he was also editing the *Courrier du Bas-Canada*, a reformist weekly paper started by Joseph Victor Delorme. In 1825, he edited the *Bibliothèque canadienne* with Viger and Labrie, followed by *L'Observateur* (a literary gazette) in 1830 and the *Magasin du Bas-Canada* in 1832. The monthly *Encyclopédie canadienne*, which he took on in 1842–3, was a new challenge which aimed to propagate a taste for art, literature and science among Canadian people.[20] 'Bibaud jeune' appraised these various journalistic pieces in the *Tableau des progrès matériels et intellectuels du Canada* (1855).[21]

The second solution was to develop a national history of Canada: all these writers attempted to write a fresh one which went back to original sources. In a letter to the 'antiquarian' Jacques Viger, Labrie said that the aim was to

20 This newspaper was 'destiné à suppléer au besoin que fait certainement sentir le manque d'un moyen efficace de propager le goût de la littérature et des sciences parmi la population franco-canadienne', *L'Encyclopédie* no. 2. This text, unlike the others, appears without its source: it may have been written by Bibaud himself.

21 See footnote no. 12.

be completely different to the historians of the past such as Pierre-François-Xavier de Charlevoix and William Smith. From January 1827, the *Bibliothèque canadienne* featured, on an increasing number of pages, 'matériaux pour l'histoire du Canada': on average stories and documents on this topic took up a third of the newspaper during 1827. Ten years later, Labrie's *History of Canada* manuscript was burnt during the rebellion. That same year, a *Catalogue d'ouvrages sur l'histoire de [... la] Nouvelle-France*,[22] compiled by G.B. Faribault, a librarian of the 'Société littéraire et historique de Québec' (founded in 1824), was published to help anyone who felt disposed to write a history of Canada 'plus complète qu'aucune de celles qui existent maintenant': in other words, more comprehensive than William Smith's (1815), which had been translated in 1825 and summarised between 1832–6 by Joseph-François Perrault.[23] Also in 1837, Bibaud brought out part one of his *Histoire du Canada sous la domination française*, continuing the historical project he had started in 1819 (but this volume contained numerous factual inaccuracies). And again in 1837, according to the *Biographical Dictionary of Canada*, François-Xavier Garneau got his historical calling. His work surpassed that of his predecessors because he used handwritten sources neglected by Faribaud's catalogue. Garneau had returned to Québec in 1833 with the intention of making his way in popular educational journalism at *L'Abeille canadienne*, a new weekly paper on the same lines as Paris's *Magasin pittoresque*. His articles promoted 'les connaissances et le goût de la lecture', but the paper failed after only two months. On 15 February 1837, *Le Canadien* included a piece by Garneau highlighting the battles Canadians were engaged in, which was as patriotic as his poems. His goal was to search the glorious past for evidence that would combat the contempt the British held for Canadians. The result of his researches is well known: the first volume of his *History of Canada* (August 1845), severely criticised by the Church but praised by the *Nouvelle Revue encyclopédique* in Paris.

We now come to the third way of constructing a nation. The long list of newspapers Bibaud was involved in is a sign of his failure. His biographers all agree that his keen determination to raise the level of education among the public did not fit well with the dry and monotonous style of his writing. However, I believe we must recognise Bibaud's genuine ambition to educate as we can see in the reviews featured in the *Bibliothèque* and the *Encyclopédie*. While many articles may only have been padding, through others Bibaud tried to develop readers' knowledge of both the geography and natural history of the

---

22   The full title is: *Catalogue d'ouvrages sur l'histoire de l'Amérique, et en particulier sur celle du Canada, de la Louisiane, de l'Acadie et autres lieux, ci-devant connus sous le nom de Nouvelle-France.*

23   The first part of Perrault's summary, *Abrégé de l'Histoire du Canada* (covering 1759–60), appeared in 1832.

mother country. The first three topics announced in a leaflet produced by the *Encyclopédie* were: 1) general history, biography and Canadian bibliography; 2) the topography, geology, mineralogy, botany and zoology 'of this country and bordering states'; and 3) progress of industry and trade. This hierarchy was not kept — with respect to literature (miscellanies, anecdotes and witticisms culled from various foreign newspapers) it was difficult to create more encyclopedic articles — but it would be unfair not to recognise what Bibaud wished to achieve. Features that provide supporting evidence include: St Maurice River and maple sugar in the first issue; Canadian woods in the second; the Ottawa River and its tributaries in the third; the fur trade in the fourth; observations about mineralogy and wild turkeys in the fifth. And it is clear he had aimed to do the same in the *Bibliothèque*, which had carried articles about agriculture (June 1826), Niagara Falls (August), mineral springs (September), Gaspé Peninsula (October), Kamouraska (November) and more. Bibaud's son may not have been objective, but he had good reason to be proud of the *Bibliothèque Canadienne*, 'le plus beau titre de gloire de mon père' (Bibaud, 1878, p. 30), for being in the vanguard of this educational literary initiative.

In 1848 *Le Répertoire national* began to draw up an inventory of Canadian literature since 1778. Most pieces were inspired by European literature. In the decade 1816–25, only one out of the 13 reproduced is an appreciation of the Canadian landscape: 'J'ai vu Chambly; j'ai vu sa fertile campagne, ses rivières, ses bois, sa triple montagne' (1816). But between 1826–45, some 20 literary pieces praised rural regions (22 texts out of 146, excluding those about the exiles and 'martyrs' of 1837).[24] They included: 'Points de vue de la descente de la montagne de Montréal' (1833, vol. I); 'L'homme de Labrador' (1837, vol. II); 'Une aventure au Labrador' (1837, II); 'La baie de Québec' (1841, II); and 'Visite à un village français sur la frontière américaine' (1842, II). Others in volume I in the same vein included: 'L'érable' (1836); 'Mon pays' (1832); 'Le voyageur' (1832); and 'Le Pont de Pierre' (1834): 'Entre deux montagnes escarpées, bordées de divers arbres, les plus beaux qu'on puisse voir, coule une rivière superbe. Les sauvages, m'a-t-on dit, lui ont donné le nom de *Scondindâio*'. And naturally we cannot leave out 'O Canada! Mon pays! Mes amours!' (1835).[25]

As for the short stories, in building a bridge between the epic French past to the present day, the Canadian tale was created. Some texts were actually

---

24 The inventory is, however, incomplete since its compiler, James Huston, was a somewhat severe critic and chose not to reproduce most of the political pieces, such as those by Papineau. There were, however, some about 'Reform and liberty', 1836, I.

25 Other descriptive passages can be found in P.-J. Olivier Chaveau's novel, *Charles Guérin*, chapters 1 and 3 part I, 6 part III, 1 part IV, and a rare description of Canadian society can be found in: 'Les boucheries. Fêtes rurales du Canada', *Répertoire* I, 1827, p. 153.

subtitled 'A Canadian legend': 'Caroline, légende canadienne' (1837, I); 'L'étranger, légende canadienne' (1837, II);[26] 'Louise, légende canadienne' (1840, II); 'Françoise Brunon. Légende de la vallée du St Laurent' (1844, III) and so on. The beginning of 'Histoire de mon oncle' (1845, III) emphasises this theme — 'C'était du temps des voyageurs, du temps que, tous les ans il partait de nos villes et de nos campagnes un essaim de jeunes Canadiens pour les *pays d'en haut*' — and so, too, does the song 'Avant tout je suis Canadien' (1832, I):

Tous les jours l'Europe se vante
Des chefs-d'œuvre de ses auteurs;
Comme elle ce pays enfante
Journaux, poètes, orateurs.
En vain le préjugé nous crie,
Cédez le pas au monde ancien:
Moi je préfère ma patrie,
Avant tout je suis Canadien.

These lines are a passionate celebration of the birth of a Canadian literature that afterwards continued to develop, emerging strongly in the mid 1840s, as L.-A. Olivier's appeal published in 1845 shows:

La culture des lettres est à son enfance parmi nous [...] Je ne prétends point faire la critique de nos écrivains mais je dois dire que peu d'entre eux ont su, suivant moi, donner à leurs œuvres une couleur originale et distinguer le caractère propre à notre littérature. Imitant au lieu de créer, ils nous peignaient les hommes de nos jours, les sciences et les mœurs de notre époque ; hommes, scènes et mœurs à peu près semblables à ceux de l'ancien monde. Erreur [...] Notre population [...] peu nombreuse, notre histoire dépouillée des grands événements qui ont agité l'Europe au commencement de ce siècle, ne leur offraient qu'un champ ingrat à cultiver [...]

Nous devons dire adieu aux hommes de nos jours, nous devons remonter aux premiers temps de notre histoire [...] Vous n'irez plus sur le bord des ruisseaux limpides épier les naïades endormies par le bruit monotones de leurs ondes ; mais vous nous peindrez de vastes nappes d'eau, dont l'œil peut à peine distinguer les limites d'avec l'azur de l'horizon [...] Vous nous montrerez, sur la cime blanche des flots, le Sauvage, assis dans son canot

26 From the novel, *L'influence d'un Livre*, by Philippe Aubert de Gaspé as, too, was the above-mentioned 'L'Homme de Labrador', chapter IX. Also featured was 'La fille du brigand, nouvelle', an excerpt from Eugène L'Écuyer's *La fille du brigand* (1844, III, p. 84).

léger fait d'écorces d'arbres […] [Telle est] la route que nous devons suivre
si nous voulons avoir une littérature à nous, une littérature canadienne.[27]

Three years later, in his introduction to the first volume of the *Répertoire
national*, Huston was able to say:

> La littérature canadienne s'affranchit lentement, il faut bien le dire,
> de tous ses langes de l'enfance. Elle laisse la voie de l'imitation pour
> s'individualiser, se nationaliser; elle avance, en chancelant encore, il est vrai,
> vers des régions nouvelles; devant elle s'ouvre un horizon et plus grand et
> plus neuf: elle commence à voir et à croire qu'elle pourra s'implanter sur le
> sol d'Amérique comme une digne bouture de cette littérature française qui
> domine et éclaire le monde.[28]

Taking into consideration the number of Canadian novels that had recently
been published, this optimism was perhaps not too extreme (if we disregard their
literary quality). They included: Joseph Doutre's *Les fiancés de 1812*, Antoine
Gérin-Lajoie's *Le jeune Latour* and Eugène L'Écuyer's *La fille du brigand*, all
published in 1844, and *Charles Guérin, roman de mœurs canadiennes* by P.-
J. Olivier Chauveau and *La terre paternelle* by Patrice Lacombe, which both
appeared in 1846.

IV

Can we conclude that Bibaud and other writers were responsible for the
evolution of Canadian literature? Probably not: these moderate intellectuals
(and rather good British subjects) certainly wished for the emergence of a
Québécoise culture, emancipated from European influence, but they did not
achieve everything they hoped for. With a degree of forced optimism, *The
Montreal Transcript* greeted the birth of the *Encyclopédie Canadienne* with this
call: 'Les talents abondent assez parmi les classes éclairées de nos co-sujets
d'origine française, pour soutenir la publication d'un ouvrage original de cette
sorte, et il serait à propos qu'une généreuse émulation les portât à encourager
une entreprise qui mérite de prospérer'.[29] But Bibaud had mixed feelings and
accused the elites of a lack of enthusiasm:

> D'après notre propre expérience et celle d'autrui, tout ce que nous pouvons
> dire avec vérité, c'est qu'il y a maintenant des centaines, des milliers, peut-
> être, de Canadiens aussi amateurs des arts et des sciences qu'on puisse l'être
> en aucun pays du monde; mais qu'il en est encore qui sont éloignés d'être

27 'Essai sur la littérature du Canada' in *Répertoire* III, 1848, p. 234.

28 *Répertoire* I, p. VI.

29 Summary: 'It would be appropriate for enlightened people of French origin to support a
publication of this kind, an enterprise which deserves to prosper'. It is no surprise that this
passage was reproduced in the *Encyclopédie* (no. 2).

> tels à un point qui causerait partout ailleurs le plus grand étonnement. Il
> en est qui sont si peu disposés à contribuer à l'extension de la typographie
> et de la bibliographie de leur pays.[30]

However, I think these writers also had a 'continental' consciousness, that is
to say both a French-speaking and an American identity, and played their
part in the emergence of Canadian literature. Michel Bibaud was interested
in estimating as closely as possible the total number of French-speaking
Americans: to an article in the *Literary Gazette* which reckoned there were
1,200,000 such souls, he countered, 'that newspaper is obviously wrong' and
came up with a total of 1,800,000:

> Hayti pas tout à fait un million d'âmes, en Guiane et dans les îles françaises
> plus de cent mille, au Bas Canada, Haut Canada et autres colonies
> britanniques, ainsi que dans les territoires sauvages appelés Pays d'en Haut,
> pas moins d'un demi million … [finally, we must add] les Français établis
> dans les grandes villes de États-Unis et dans les divers états de l'Amérique
> ci-devant espagnole. [31]

The *Encyclopédie Canadienne*'s first article[32] asked the same question and
concluded that there were two million in Canada, Louisiana and the West Indies,
not including French-speaking people from France, Belgium, Switzerland,
Savoy and Piedmont, who lived in the US and 'formerly Spanish or Portuguese
colonies'. This population count was a way of voicing a continental solidarity
and also a French-American identity.

Bibaud cited the following newspapers most frequently in the *Encyclopédie*:
Le Canadien, the *Gazette de Québec*, *L'Aurore des Canadas*, the *Bytown Gazette*,
the *Journal Américain* and the *Courrier des États-Unis*. While these were the
primary sources,[33] Canadian newspapers were occasionally featured (*Quebec
Mercury*, *Montreal Transcript*, *Cornwall Observer*, *Montreal Gazette*, *Bathurst
Courier*) and articles were also included from *The Whig* (Yazoo, Missouri),
the *Knoxville Post* (Tennessee), the *Albany Atlas*, the *Journal de Baltimore*, the
Rochester Advertiser, the *Illinois Register*, the *Michigan White Pigeon Gazette*, the
Abeille de la Nouvelle-Orléans and so on.

One final point: coverage of history topics was significantly greater in the
Encyclopédie than in the *Bibliothèque*. The former review not only highlighted
Canada but also 'Antiquités Américaines' and in this broader scenario Bibaud
wrote columns called 'American biography', devoted to the First Nations such

---

30 *Encyclopédie*, p. 390.

31 *Bibliothèque*, July 1826, p. 68.

32 'La langue française', *Encyclopédie*, 1842.

33 Unlikely though it may seem, titles in this category also included: *L'indépendant* (from
    Brussels), *L'observateur Belge* and *L'industriel alsacien*.

as: Siquahyam (the Cherokee tribe), Ahasistari (Huron), Piskaret (Algonquin) and Garakonthie (Iroquois). But Bibaud was just one part of an intellectual movement we can discern in Huston's *Répertoire*:

> 1826: 'Chanson du voyageur Canadien', **traduction de la chanson anglaise de Moore,**[34] or the 'verses travellers are thought to have sung when they travelled along the Ottawa River to the Grand-Portage'.
>
> 1827: 'L'Iroquoise, Histoire ou nouvelle historique'.
>
> 1831: 'L'Iroquoise, Hymne de guerre', which was 'translated from a war anthem sung by ancient heroes sprung from [American] soil [...] their poetry was as great and noble as the country they lived in'.
>
> 1840: 'Chant de guerre d'un Huron' and 'Le dernier Huron'.
>
> 1845: 'Le sacrifice du Sauvage'.

Other circumstances contributed to the fact that these efforts to build an original French-American identity were not a complete success. Canadian society had become more rural since the Conquest, increasing from 75 per cent in 1760 to 85–90 per cent in 1825–45, and the population had spread, having colonised areas as remote as Lac-Saint-Jean, for example. That new sociological trend furthered the emergence of a rural, catholic, patriotic, conservative literature and identity. *La terre paternelle* by Patrice Lacombe (1846) was the first example of this 'littérature du terroir'. But a letter Bibaud published in the *Encyclopédie* (no. 2) observed: 'Il faut peu compter sur notre classe agricole, qui ne saurait avoir de goût pour tout ce qui regarde l'éducation en général, parce qu'elle n'en connaît pas encore le prix; mais j'espère qu'au moins tout ce qu'il y a de Canadiens instruits [...] s'empressera d'encourager votre production'.[35] According to historical monographs (Verrette, 1979, Veilleux, 1981, Hamelin, 1982), Canadian literacy levels would have fallen[36] between the Conquest (more precisely the Seven Years War) and the early 19th century, or even the 1840s, before the establishment of a school system could take significant effect.[37]

---

34 My emphasis. Note a common interest here between French- and English-speaking writers.

35 In short: The Canadian intellectual could not rely upon rural people as they did not understand the worth of education.

36 Deduced from signatures in parish registers, a somewhat unreliable method.

37 In Québec, the decline was especially marked in the female population: 37% were able to sign in 1790–9, 28% in 1840–9, with similar statistics being obtained for the 'Côte du Sud' (the right bank of the lower St Lawrence), especially in Catholic homes (43% in 1750–9, 29% in 1840–9). But, as Veilleux remarked, there were major differences between parishes. In 1830, Bibaud calculated that 2,000 Canadians could write in French: undoubtedly a close estimate. But being unable to write did not mean that people could not read as collective

Almanacs like the one in the *Minerve*, sold in the Trois-Rivières and Montréal regions with a circulation of thousands, were the only publications, along with devotional books, that country people were able to obtain. Lemoyne's study of the inventories of countryside and city homes found that the most popular were Abbé Huvey's *Formulaire de prière* (1779) the *Journée du Chrétien* prayer book from the same period and the famous but even older *Imitation de Jésus-Christ*, first published in 1659.[38] Catholicism was the only thing shared by all Canadian people, cultivated or not, especially after the revolt of 1837–8: the third volume of Garneau's *History of Canada* (1849), disarmed the initial criticisms of the Church by emphasising the link between faith and nation. In 1866, Abbé Henri-Raymond Casgrain wrote:

> notre littérature sera grave, méditative, spiritualiste, religieuse,
> évangélisatrice comme nos missionnaires, généreuse comme nos martyrs,
> énergique et persévérante comme nos pionniers d'autrefois; et en même
> temps elle sera largement découpée, comme nos vastes fleuves, nos
> larges horizons, notre grandiose nature, mystérieuse comme les échos
> de nos immenses et impénétrables forêts [...] Mais surtout elle sera
> essentiellement croyante, religieuse; telle sera sa forme caractéristique,
> son expression; sinon elle ne vivra pas, elle se tuera elle-même. (Casgrain,
> 1866, pp. 25–6.

This reinforced what Casgrain had said earlier (p. 9): 'Why should we lose hope of establishing an intellectual colony for France as we have created a new France on this continent?' Moreover, poets and novelists had followed L.-A. Olivier's previous recommendations: 'we must say farewell to the men of today, we must go back to the early days of our history' and celebrate major events, whether happy or tragic, and through them the Discoverer, the Settler (such as Dollard-des-Ormeaux) and the Martyr (such as missionaries, Acadians or Patriots). These are examples of necessary resistance within the contexts of the Rebellion and the influence of French Romanticism, but working along these lines also allowed Canadian writers to be free from France henceforth and to stand on equal terms with French authors.

The period 1820–40 was, then, a significant moment in the intellectual history of the French-speaking middle class and was probably also the story of a generation: Bibaud was born in 1782, Labrie in 1784, Viger in 1787 and

---

reading was frequently practised (there were approximately ten listeners per each newspaper subscriber during the French Revolution). The real problem, according to Labonté, was the gap between Anglophones and Canadians: Québec death inventories from the 1820s show that 65% of Anglophones owned books, but only 38% of Canadians.

38 Incidentally, *Imitation de Jésus-Christ* was also ubiquitous at that time in the homes of the lower classes in far-away Le Havre.

Faribaud in 1789.[39] They were too young to be concerned about the French Revolution and its reverberations throughout Canada, but old enough to be disillusioned by this new and complex country, and they had grown up in a world where Britain was less an enemy than a protector. Moving ever further away from France, the Canadian intelligentsia tried to overcome the ambiguities between nationalism and class consciousness, French-speaking and bilingualism, old France and Britain, reformism and conservatism, Europe and America. Later on, having realised their loyalty had been unsuccessful, they were forced to ask 'what is a Canadian?' They tried to provide an answer and build a national identity separate from Europe. All things considered, their attempt made possible the birth of an original Canadian literature. Canadian writers did not have to imitate Europe any more: they had to get inspiration from '[their] huge rivers and [their] big mountains', the Savage and the wilderness.[40] They had to feel American.

REFERENCES

Bibaud, François-Maximilien ('Bibaud jeune', Michel's son) (1855) *Tableau historique des progrès matériels et intellectuels du Canada* and *Les institutions de l'Histoire du Canada ou Annales canadiennes jusqu'à l'an MDCCCXIX* (Montréal).

Bibaud, Michel (ed.) (1825–30) *Bibliothèque canadienne* (Montréal).

Bibaud, Michel (ed.) (1842–3) *Encyclopédie canadienne* (Montréal).

Bibaud, Michel (1837) 3-volume *Histoire du Canada sous la domination française* (Montreal; 2nd edn. 1843; repr. New York: 1968).

Bibaud, Michel (1844) *Histoire du Canada et des Canadiens, sous la domination anglaise,* [1760–1830] (Montréal; repr. East Ardsley, England and New York: 1968).

Bibaud, Jean Gaspard (ed.) [Michel's son] (1878) *Histoire du Canada et des Canadiens, sous la domination anglaise,* [1830–37] (Montréal).

Bujila, Bernardine (1960) 'Michel Bibaud's *Encyclopédie canadienne*', *Culture* no. 21 (Québec), pp. 117–32.

Casgrain, Abbé Henri-Raymond (1866) 'Le mouvement littéraire au Canada', *Le Foyer Canadien,* (Québec: January).

39 Note that, apart from Lacombe (who was a little older), the novelists of the 1840s, such as L'Écuyer or Chauveau, belonged to another generation born in the 1820s.
40 'Essai sur la littérature au Canada', *Répertoire* III, 1848, pp. 236–8.

Claxton, Patricia (ed. and trans.) (1980) *Lower Canada 1791–1840* [comprising Ouellet's works listed below], The Canadian Centenary Series (Ottawa: Carleton Library).

de Lagrave, Jean-Paul (1944) *L'époque de Voltaire au Canada* (Montréal).

Frégault, Guy (1944–5) 'Michel Bibaud, historien loyaliste', *L'Action universitaire* (Montréal).

Faribault, Georges-Barthélemi (compiler) (1837) *Catalogue d'ouvrages sur l'histoire de l'Amérique, et en particulier sur celle du Canada, de la Louisiane, de l'Acadie et autres lieux, ci-devant connus sous le nom de Nouvelle-France* (Québec: W. Cowan).

Galarneau, Claude (1970) *La France devant l'opinion canadienne, 1760–1815* (Québec).

Huston, James (compiler/publisher) 1848–50 *Répertoire national ou recueil de littérature canadienne* 4 vols. (Montréal).

Garneau, François-Xavier (1845–8) *History of Canada* 3 vols. (Québec: suppl. 1852).

Hamelin, Pierre (1982) 'L'alphabétisation de la Côte du Sud 1680–1869', MA thesis (Montréal: Université Laval).

Huvey, Abbé Jérôme (1779) *Formulaire de prière*, 1st edn. (Québec).

Labonté, Gilles (1986) 'Les bibliothèques privées à Québec 1820–1829', MA thesis (Montréal: Université Laval).

Labrie, Jacques (1827) *Les premiers rudimens de la constitution britannique* (Montréal).

Lacombe, Patrice (1846) *La terre paternelle* (Montréal: most recent edn. 1981).

Lemoyne, Réjean (1981) 'Le marché du livre à Québec, 1764–1839', MA thesis (Montréal: Université Laval).

Malchelosse, Gérard (1945) *Michel Bibaud* (Montréal).

Ouellet, Fernand (1966) *Histoire économique et sociale du Québec, 1760–1850* (Montréal).

Ouellet, Fernand (1976) *Bas-Canada, 1791–1840: changements structuraux et crise* (Montréal).

Perrault, Joseph-François, *Abrégé de l'histoire du Canada. Première partie: depuis sa découverte jusqu'à sa conquête par les Anglais en 1759 et 1760*, 5 vols. (Québec: 1831–6).

Perrault, Pauline (1951) 'Bio-bibliographie de Michel Bibaud, journaliste, poète, historien', thesis (Montréal: Université de Montréal).

Raban, Louis-François (1826) *Petite biographie des Députés de France* (Paris).

Schonberger, V.L. (Vincent) (1977) 'Le journalisme littéraire de Michel Bibaud', *Revue de l'Université d'Ottawa*, no. 47, pp. 488–505.

Sicotte, L.-W. (Louis-Wilfrid) (1908) *Michel Bibaud*, (Montréal).

Simard, Sylvain (ed.) (1991) *La Révolution française au Canada français* (Ottawa).

Tessier, Xavier (ed.) (1828) *Journal des Sciences Naturelles* (New York).

Tousignant, Claude (1974) 'Michel Bibaud: sa vie, son œuvre et son combat politique', *Recherches sociographiques* no. 15 (Québec), pp. 21–30.

Veilleux, Christine (1981) 'L'évolution de l'alphabétisation dans le comté de Portneuf, 1690–1849', MA thesis (Montréal: Université Laval).

Verrette, Michel (1979) 'L'alphabétisation de la population de la ville de Québec 1750–1849', MA thesis (Montréal: Université Laval).

5

QUEBEC, ACADIA AND LOUISIANA: THE IMPACT OF REUNIONS AND GATHERINGS

Barry Jean Ancelet

This chapter explores the influence of the gatherings and reunions between Louisiana Cajuns and their cousins from Québec and the Acadian maritime provinces in Canada (New Brunswick, Nova Scotia and Prince Edward Island). Beginning with the bicentennial celebration of the *Grand Dérangement* in 1955, they encompass the *Rencontres des Peuples Francophones* in Québec City and the various manifestations of the *Congrès Mondial Acadien*. The effect of these gatherings confirms the concepts proposed by the members of Projet Louisiane in *Du continent perdu à l'archipel retrouvé*, (Louder & Waddell, 1983) especially concerning the arts and culture.

In 1955, the Acadians in Canada and the Cajuns of Louisiana, in a sense twins separated at adolescence by the events of 1755, found themselves reunited to celebrate the bicentennial of the *Grand Dérangement*. One might initially find it curious that they would be celebrating what was arguably the most traumatic event in their history, but the message of 1955 was above all one of victory for a people that had survived and preserved their identity against all odds and now wanted to celebrate their history and culture. In truth, they had done more than survive; rather, they had thrived in the various contexts in which they were living. The result of this encounter for the Cajuns of Louisiana was to reopen the lines of communication with the isolated islands of the Acadian archipelago from which they had remained separated for too long.

Louisiana State Senator Dudley LeBlanc took with him a delegation of young Cajun girls dressed in Evangeline costumes. This was not his first visit to the Acadians in Canada as he had organised several other similar expeditions in 1930 and 1936. His goal was to bring back together the two poles of Acadian society. These initial forays served to reunite the descendants of the Acadian diaspora. They also served to further LeBlanc's own political career. His reputation was based largely on his support for the Acadian cause and for the preservation of the French language in Louisiana, as well as for his efforts to improve conditions for the elderly and the poor. The 1955 trip was emotionally charged for those who discovered that many had managed to survive and even thrive despite the historical pressures, and often in remarkably similar social and economic contexts, based on a common knack for innovating solutions and adapting to conditions.

Several more trips and a few exchange programmes ensued, but nothing that approached the mainstream. In Cajun Louisiana, the most important consequence of the bicentennial reunion was a new awareness, especially among the elite, that there were possible connections to a larger Acadian reality and to a wide French-speaking world. Thomas Arceneaux, Dean of the School of Agriculture at the then Southwestern Louisiana Institute (now the University of Louisiana at Lafayette) and an Acadian activist, designed a new flag for Louisiana Acadians, which everyone took care to keep in its proper place alongside national and state flags. During the 1960s, certain members of the community began discussing in discrete groups the effects of Americanisation and the political and social consequences of the 'melting pot'. The latter represented systematic efforts over more than a century to assimilate the Cajuns, especially through stigmatisation of their French language.

This ongoing debate, inspired in 1966 by Raymond Rogers, was led by the members of the *Comité de l'héritage français* (formed in 1965 to organise the bicentennial celebration of the arrival of the Acadians in Louisiana). These members included Wade Martin, Allen Babineaux and later James Domengeaux (Baillargeon, 2007). All this eventually led to the creation of the Council for the Development of French in Louisiana (CODOFIL) in 1968. Ironically, this now constituted an official agency of the same State of Louisiana that had officially banished French from its school systems in 1916. That same year, far-flung descendants of the Acadian diaspora met once again to celebrate the documentary film, *Les Acadiens de la dispersion*.[1] The director and several of those featured in the film, including a young Edith Butler, came to Louisiana for a Cajun country premier. The reunions were gaining momentum and a certain popularity.

In its early days, CODOFIL represented the political and academic inclinations of its founders but it was not long before the Council began to develop more popular, grass roots approaches, which eventually came to the fore in a very public way in 1974 with the creation of the Cajun Music Festival. This event was the result of at least ten years of lobbying by American folklorists who were actively challenging the melting pot, especially Ralph Rinzler, who had discovered Louisiana Cajun and Creole music in 1964 while doing fieldwork for the Newport Folk Festival. Rinzler was in turn guided by his mentor, Alan Lomax, a member of the Newport festival board who had

1   *Les Acadiens de la dispersion*, dir. Léonard Forêt, National Film Board of Canada, 1968.

himself discovered Louisiana Cajun and Creole music while doing fieldwork with his father John for the Library of Congress in 1934.

Based on Rinzler's fieldwork, the Newport board invited a trio of Cajun musicians to perform at the 1964 festival. This initial performance opened the door for many others, at Newport and at other folk festivals across America, as Cajun music went from a little known regional genre to finding a place at the table of America's folk music styles. Rinzler, who served as consultant and master of ceremonies for the Louisiana festival in 1974, had become Director of Folklife Programs at the Smithsonian Institution in Washington, DC. He continued to invite Cajun and Creole musicians to perform at the Smithsonian's Festival of American Folklife, featuring them as a model for cultural self-preservation in the American context. In 1976, Cajuns and Creoles were an important part of the American Bicentennial version of the Smithsonian Festival. Rinzler's strategy consisted of reuniting ethnic and cultural groups from various parts of America with their counterparts from their countries of origin. In this case, Cajuns were reunited with folk performers from France, Québec, Canada's Acadian provinces, the French-influenced north-east and Old Illinois country, and even Haiti. Folk singers and musicians from Louisiana discovered that they shared many songs and stories with their French, French Canadian and French American colleagues. Participants in this festival experiment found also that they were able to communicate well enough in their various interrelated French dialects, which in most cases had been stigmatised by educational systems that had long sought to standardise the language (see Ancelet, 2004–5, 2007, 2008 and Ancelet (ed.), 1980).

After the *révolutions tranquilles* and not so *tranquilles* of the 1960s and 1970s in Québec, certain activists became interested in the phenomenon of living in French in North America, perhaps so that they would not feel so all alone. Toward the end of the 1960s, the Québec government opened an official delegation in Lafayette, Louisiana. The presence of Québec's *délégué* and eventually of dozens of Québécois teachers, who came to teach French alongside teachers from France and Belgium in the new second language programmes developed by CODOFIL, had a profound effect on the Louisiana context on a number of levels. The teachers from Québec already had a notion of what it meant to live in French in North America, as well as how the French language could serve to express the vernacular. Moreover, many among them had considerable experience in what was called *animation culturelle* and were active outside their classrooms, organising literary readings and even a new popular theatre, the Théâtre Cadien.

Québec's first delegate, Léo LeBlanc, a transplanted Acadian, contributed subtly but effectively to the establishment, in 1974, of the first music festival. In 1975, back in Québec, a group of activists including the filmmakers André

Gladu and Michel Brault, who were in the process of producing the extensive documentary series, *Le son des Français d'Amérique* (1976),[2] helped to organise *La Veillée des Veillées*, a concert in Montréal that gathered musicians and singers from various parts of the French-speaking world. Taking their places alongside performers from France, Québec, Ontario and the Acadian Maritimes were Zachary Richard, Marc Savoy, D. L. Menard, Lionel Leleux and Dieudonné Montoucet from Louisiana. This encounter launched a series of exchanges that has lasted for several generations.

André Gladu also met Revon Reed, a Louisiana French teacher and cultural activist who had worked with Rinzler in the 1960s; the two went on to collaborate on *Lache pas la patate,* the first book in Cajun French, published in Montréal in 1976, originally conceived as an exchange of letters between the two correspondents (hence the original title, *Cher André*) (Reed, 1976). A number of Québecois, Acadian and Cajun musicians were subsequently invited to folk festivals in Québec, New Brunswick, Nova Scotia and Louisiana. Zachary Richard has gone on to become a star in Québec and France. In 1978, two of the *Veillée* participants, Montoucet and Leleux, played at Québec's *Festival d'Été*, as well as New Brunswick's *Frolic des Acadiens* and Nova Scotia's *Festival Acadien de Clare*, opening the door for other musicians. In 1979, supported by the Government of Québec, Louisiana's *Festival de musique acadienne* began featuring musicians from Québec, including Philippe Bruneau and Gilles Loisier, la Grande Roue, Jocelyn Bérubé, la Bottine Souriante, and Alain LaMontagne. And, in 1982, the tricentennial of the claiming of the Louisiana colony by the Cavalier de la Salle in 1682 was celebrated with the inclusion of musicians from Québec (Rêve du Diable), New Brunswick (1755), Nova Scotia (Les Tymeux de la Baie), Missouri (Charlie Pasha), the Dakotas (the Eddie King group), and Haiti (a ra-ra group).

Beginning in 1986, Lafayette's other celebration, *Festival International de Louisiane,* expanded on this model, featuring musicians from all over the French-speaking world, including Europe, Africa, the West Indies, and the Indian Ocean, as well as North America. These experiments have had the effect of demonstrating to Louisiana Cajuns and Creoles that we are neither alone nor strange, simply separated from our counterparts in space and time. We also came to understand that we had evolved, influenced by the *mélange* and the cultural fusion that are at the heart of our region.

Along with the University of Louisiana at Lafayette, CODOFIL has also served as a contact point for other communities seeking to reunite the far-flung societies of the North American French archipelago. In June and July of 1978, the Québec government invited a Louisiana delegation to participate

---

2   *Le son des Français d'Amérique,* 26 part series, dir. André Gladu and Michel Brault, Nanouk Films, 1976.

in the *Rencontre des Francophones d'Amérique,* organised by Marcel Dubé and sponsored by the Secrétariat Permanent des Peuples Francophones d'Amérique and the Conseil de la Vie Française en Amérique. It included a conference at which a number of academics and activists from Louisiana presented papers on the current state of the French language and culture in the region. As part of the *Rencontre,* Dubé also organised an evening of literary readings, *Paroles et Musique,* partly to celebrate Québec's 370th anniversary. It featured the début of Claude Léveillé's *Concerto pour Hélène,* in honour of Hélène Boulé, the wife of Québec City's founder, Samuel de Champlain. That evening the same stage featured several francophone poets, including Michelle Lalonde and Raoul Duguay from Québec, Herménégilde Chiasson from Acadian New Brunswick and Jean Arceneaux from Cajun Louisiana.

This experience inspired Arceneaux to collaborate in 1979 with Cajun singer Zachary Richard, in Louisiana, on producing a version of *Paroles et Musique*; the two eventually gathered together some of the poetry featured during that evening in *Cris sur le bayou* (Ancelet (ed.), 1980), the first anthology to be produced of contemporary French Cajun and Creole poetry since the turn of the 20th century. This first collection, published in Montréal (Editions Intermède), was followed by several others, published in Louisiana (Editions de la Nouvelle Acadie), in New Brunswick (Editions d'Acadie and Editions Perce-Neige), in Québec (Les Intouchables and Louise Courteau), and in France (ACE). Important contacts were also established between authors from Québec (including Gaston Miron), from New Brunswick (Gérald LeBlanc, Rose Després, Dyane Léger, among others) and from France (Bernard Mounier), which eventually resulted in a series of exchanges and lectures. These inserted Louisiana's young French-language literature into the larger context of the French-speaking world, as Cajun and Creole authors participated in literary events sponsored by a number of Salons du Livre throughout French Canada, alongside such luminaries as Gaston Miron, Antonine Maillet, and Raphaël Confiant among many others.

In 1982, France celebrated the 350th anniversary of the departure to the New World of those who would become the Acadians by bringing together first in La Rochelle, then at Centre Pompidou in Paris, Acadian and Cajun poets and singers. This reunion enabled a continuation of the newly revived discourse — after long separation — that had been generated by the previous reunions. Finding themselves together in France, both sides — far from their respective homelands but once again in the land of their common origins — intensified the lines of communication. Discovering their cultural expression validated in the context of France added to the impact of the experience.

During the 1980s, Québec began to rethink its role in francophone New America. For some, the concept of *francophonie* was inextricably linked to the problematic situation of linguistic minorities and thus did not apply to Québec, where French-speakers were in the overwhelming majority. During this same period, Québec was involved in trying to achieve a position of quasi-independence, especially in its economic and diplomatic relations. In 1992, the government of Québec withdrew its delegation from Lafayette, preferring to concentrate its efforts in more commercially viable potential centres such as Atlanta. Cultural exchanges with Québec virtually ended; the number of French teachers from Québec also plummeted from well over two dozen in the 1980s to barely a handful following the closing of these avenues.

On the other hand, the cultural connections between *l'Acadie du Nord* and *l'Acadie Tropicale* continued to grow. In April of 1978, shortly before the first *Rencontre des Peuples Francophones d'Amérique* in Québec, the University of Moncton had organised an academic conference on the Acadian diaspora, the *Colloque sur l'Acadie,* ironically in the same year that Michel Roy's *L'Acadie perdue* was published (Roy, 1978). Scholars from across the academic spectrum, including history, ethnology, sociology, economics, linguistics, political science, law and literary studies, gathered to discuss what had become of Acadia and the Acadians following the deportation in 1755. This was, in a sense, a follow-up to the reunions of 1955, but with an academic rather than a political focus. This did not preclude, however, a serious discussion of the implications of Acadian identity at this point close to the end of the 20th century. This multidisciplinary discussion focused on those elements that seemed to have survived among the descendants of the exiled Acadians, as well as those that had obviously changed, recognising both developments as critical to understanding the contemporary situation. Some of the participating scholars maintained the contacts that they developed there, but at this stage there was not yet a popular dimension.

This changed in 1994 with the first *Congrès Mondial Acadien,* which also took place in Moncton. The CMA website explains how it originated:

> It was in the context of a lobster supper organised by the *Société acadienne de l'Alberta* in October, 1988, that Acadian Jean-Marie Nadeau proposed the idea of organising a gathering of Acadians from all over the world. André Boudreau, a native of New Brunswick living in Edmonton, decided to take on the challenge of realising Mr. Nadeau's idea. [translated from the original French][3]

The Cyberacadie website describes the events that ensued:

> The World Acadian Congress 1994, which took place August 12–22, 1994, in the Acadia-Beauséjour region (south-eastern New Brunswick, Canada), was the largest gathering of Acadian people since the events of the *Grand Dérangement* (1755–62). More than 300,000 people

3   CMA-Caraquet 2009 website: www.cma.2009

participated in the 69 family reunions, in the academic conferences, in the festival of Acadian film and theatre and in the various concerts, as well as in the many other cultural events of all kinds.

In this International Year of the Family (1994), never was there a better time for family reunions. The importance of finding ourselves among family and of re-establishing ties that have been broken for too long is an important part of *Retrouvailles 94*.

There is no doubt that the World Acadian Congress has affected Acadia. It has permitted Acadians everywhere to regroup and renew ties, to reflect on the long voyage that we have been on for nearly 400 years, to regain confidence in ourselves and to dream of the future. [translated from the original French][4]

Louisiana Cajuns participated in an important way in the Congress and its cultural events that gathered Acadians en masse and in a very public way. During the academic conferences, important and thorny questions were raised concerning assimilation of various sorts including: the issue of Acadians in Québec; the importance of the French language as an identity marker; the social, economic and political factors facing Acadians today; and our chances for survival in the future. In the area of popular culture, the family reunions and a huge *tintamarre* (noise-making procession) became the symbolic focus of the Congress. Thousands of the descendants of Acadians who were exiled, or had survived by hiding in the woods for decades after the deportation, came together and took to the streets in a highly public celebration of their Acadian identity, making a joyous racket and carrying innumerable representations of the Acadian flag, proceeding eventually to the site of a grand closing concert that featured Edith Butler, Zachary Richard and 1755, among others, on an ultra-modern stage for an event that was broadcast on national television across Canada. I was among the crowd and can attest that Acadian pride was boosted considerably. The most obvious result, in my opinion, was the solidarity generated by the reunions and in the power of the public expression of this society that is sometimes considered fragile, but that has endured despite the powerful forces allayed against it. We witnessed the birth of friendship and kinship ties that continue to thrive despite the distance between our respective homelands.

Before the first Congress had ended, it was decided that the event was worth repeating. The second CMA took place in 1999 in Louisiana, as part of the tricentennial celebration of the founding of the Louisiana colony by the French in 1699. This second Congress essentially followed the model of the first, with an academic conference, cultural events and, most importantly,

4   Cyberacadie.com

family reunions. Fewer Acadians from the Canadian maritime provinces made the trip to participate than was hoped, due in no small part to the fact that this conference, like the first, was anchored to 15 August, the 'national' Acadian holiday. This detracted from the Congress' potential for success for several reasons. First, the Canadian Acadians are used to celebrating 15 August in their own communities, while this date has no particular significance in Louisiana. Second, this time of year is notoriously hot in Louisiana, even for those who live there and are relatively acclimatised. Many northern Acadians expressed concern about their ability to handle the heat. And third, all of the Cajun sub-regions of Louisiana — from Lafourche and Terrebonne along the south-eastern coast, to Avoyelles in central Louisiana, to Cameron and Calcasieu along the Texas border — insisted on participating, requiring a complex programme of events that was difficult to negotiate and impossibly spread out. Despite all of these challenges, thousands of Acadians participated in this second mass rally. Louisiana Cajuns, already familiar with the festival procession called Mardi Gras, were introduced to the *tintamarre,* which had been a focal point of the first Congress. The closing concert once again brought together musicians and singers from throughout the Acadian diaspora and once again produced moments of high emotion and great solidarity.

The third CMA took place in 2004 in Nova Scotia, a historic return to the birthplace of the Acadian people on the occasion of the 400th anniversary of the founding of the Acadian colony by Champlain in 1604. The Nova Scotian context posed several challenges, mainly caused by geography. The repatriation conditions of the Acadians, who appealed to return to the colony after the French and Indian Wars, prevented them from settling together in one place and especially from putting down roots anywhere near their original lands, taken from them as a result of the exile. Today, Nova Scotian Acadians are isolated in a few areas along Saint Mary's Bay in the south-west, around Pubnico on the Atlantic side of Yarmouth, in Ile Madame on the north-eastern part of the peninsula and around Cheticamp on Cape Breton Island far to the north, with the largest number now living and working in the Halifax metropolitan area, including many who have lost their native French language. But there are virtually none in the Port-Royal area where Champlain initially built his Habitation in 1604, nor in the Annapolis Valley, including Grand Pré where the exile started in 1755, nor in Beaubassin or the other regions where the deportation effort continued throughout 1762, despite the resistance of a few Acadian fighters led by Beausoleil Broussard.

Ironically, the fewest Acadians live in the sites of greatest historical interest. Moreover, to get from one contemporary Acadian settlement to another necessitates travelling considerable distances through vast Anglo-Canadian regions. Keenly aware of the Congress and its potential to generate cultural tourism, the people from these areas came forward to participate in the events, producing phenomena that would have been hard to imagine only a few years before, such as an Acadian flag displayed outside a bed-and-breakfast in Lawrencetown (which bears the same name as the British governor who deported the Acadians). At the academic conference organised for this third Congress, named Vision 2020, participants continued the debates launched at the first CMA in 1994 concerning Acadian identity, geography and potential for the future.

According to Wikipedia:

> The third congress, in 2004, was held jointly by several Nova Scotia communities in the ancestral Acadian region and celebrated the 400th anniversary of the arrival of the first French-speaking settlers in Canada. As in the previous gatherings, musical festivals and theatrical productions displayed Acadian culture and academics debated the meaning of Acadia in the 21st century. Debates included the best ways of preserving Acadian culture in an overwhelmingly English area, and what exactly an Acadian is in 2004. Some Acadians in the Maritimes do not recognise more recent immigrants as true Acadians. There was also a debate about whether the descendants of Acadians, who do not speak French, qualify.[5]

The *tintamarre,* now a signature feature of the Congresses, was once again featured along Baie Sainte-Marie, reversing the lessons of the past that had cautioned against doing anything to attract attention to the community. Even before the CMA 2004, a cooperative spirit had developed between Nova Scotian Acadians and Louisiana Cajuns, who share similar minority status, especially through the Université Sainte-Anne's French immersion programmes and its Acadian Studies Institut, where hundreds of Louisiana Cajun students have studied French and Acadian culture over the years. Conversely, several Acadians from Nova Scotia have earned MAs/PhDs in the graduate programme in Francophone Studies at the University of Louisiana at Lafayette. Scholars from both academic communities participate in research projects and centres, such as the latter's Center for Louisiana Studies and the University of Sainte-Anne's Groupe de recherches en études acadiennes, as well as a joint effort to explore how to integrate variable vernacular French into the educational system at all levels.

Contact with Québec has continued, especially in the area of cultural exchanges, as well as pedagogical and other academic joint projects, including participation in the *Base de données lexicographiques panfrancophone,* directed by Claude Poirier at the Université Laval. During a recent meeting of the *Biennale*

---

5   http://en.wikipedia.org/wiki/Acadian_World_Congress. Further information about
    Congress 3 is available at www.acadian.org/congres3.html

de la Langue Française en Amérique in Moncton (2007), the Government of Québec announced a reconsideration of its official position within the francophone community of North America, resuming its leadership role. In 2008, the Québec Government delegation in Atlanta joined Lafayette's *Festivals Acadiens et Créoles* in celebrating the 400th anniversary of the founding of Québec in 1608, sponsoring a special performance by Zachary Richard and his group of musicians, who were mostly from la Belle Province. The organisers of CMA 2009 in Caraquet, New Brunswick, also joined the festival, sponsoring a reunion performance of the legendary Acadian group, 1755.

The Caraquet CMA 2009 website outlines its mission statement:

> The World Acadian Congress is a grand gathering of Acadians from all over the world. It takes place every five years and the next one will be in the Acadian peninsula of north-eastern New Brunswick. It will be a unique opportunity to reunite with Acadian cousins from all over the world in order to celebrate our common history.

> The mission of the World Acadian Congress was defined as follows: 'To develop more direct connections between Acadians from all over the world.' For the Acadian people, it is very important to be able to exchange ideas, to meet extended family and relations, to hear of new innovations on any number of subjects and to debate points of common interest.[6]

As Carol Doucet put it, the goal of the Congress in general is to:

> Provide an opportunity for Acadians of the diaspora to be able to have a time and a place to meet at least once each five years. This is the main reason that the World Acadian Congress was founded in the early 1990s. With the very first Congress, which took place in New Brunswick in 1994, in the southeast and in County Kent, many Louisiana Cajuns came to Acadie du Nord to re-establish contact with their cousins. 'Durable ties were created and reinforced in 1994, and again in 1999, and in 2004, and the year 2009 will not be an exception', according to Congress President Rioux. (Doucet, 2008)

The themes of the Congresses and of their attendant conferences reflect the consistent desire of the organisers to gather the people and to consider their future: *Retrouvailles 94* and *L'Acadie en 2004* (1994); *Un peuple, deux drapeaux* and *Acadie/Acadies: A travers des frontières* (1999); *Retour au berceau* and *Vision 20/20* (2004); *L'Acadie rassemblent* and *L'Acadie en mouvement* (2009). The theme song of the first CMA in 1994, by Johnny Comeau, also represented a call to gather: '*Acadie de nos coeurs, enfin c'est ton heure. Tes enfants reviennent dans tes bras …*' (Acadia of our hearts, finally it's your time. Your children are

6   www.cma.2009

coming back to your arms …). In 1999, Waylon Thibodeaux continued the tradition with *'Si longtemps séparés …'* (So long separated …). In 2004, the provocatively named Acadian musical group, Grand Dérangement, issued an invitation to everyone with *'Je reviens au berceau de l'Acadie …'* (I'm coming home to the birthplace of Acadia …).

It is interesting to note that the spirit of these gatherings and the results of the experiences they create derive not only from the conferences, the festivals, the Congress meetings, the publications or the films. The gatherings take place before and after the officially organised events, improvised by people who meet each other and eventually develop affective relationships with their counterparts. Separated so long by time and distance, as well as by ignorance, we knew virtually nothing about each other. In this day and age, these three obstacles can be easily overcome and should not continue to separate us. We are not just limited to making the occasional road or air trip across this vast continent, 'island' hopping through this cultural and linguistic archipelago, but can now also travel through cyberspace to maintain virtual contact with each other. The various francophone peoples of North America can, according to our own interests and means, pursue and maintain contacts with those we meet through these gatherings. Moisy Baudoin, a working man from Delcambre, Louisiana, articulated the experience of many during an interview he gave to Germaine Comeau for a documentary on the Acadians of Baie Sainte-Marie. She asked him, 'Why do you travel so far to come to Acadia?' He answered without hesitation, 'We like the lobster and the scallops and the festivals and all the rest, but really, it's the people. It's the people that we love. They welcome us with open arms like family. You don't find that just anywhere.' This feeling of belonging, of attachment, finally makes us feel as though we are part of a larger context. In this, there is a powerful sense of validation.

REFERENCES

Ancelet, Barry Jean (ed.) (1980) *Cris sur le bayou: Naissance d'une poésie acadienne et créole en Louisiane* (Montréal: Éditions Intermède).

Ancelet, Barry Jean (2004–5) 'Valoriser la variabilité pour préserver une identité linguistique', *Port Acadie: Revue Interdisciplinaire en études acadiennes,* vol. 6–7 (Autumn–Spring), pp. 21–40.

Ancelet, Barry Jean (2007) 'Negotiating the Mainstream: The Cajuns and Creoles in Louisiana', *French Review,* vol. 80, no. 6 (May), pp. 1235–55.

Ancelet, Barry Jean (2008) *Francophonies d'Amérique* (account of the Biénnale Amérique de la Langue Française), vol. 26 (Autumn).

Baillargeon, Marie-Ginette (2007) 'Un mariage de convenance: L'influence du Québec sur l'essor du Conseil pour le Développement du Français en Louisiana', Ph.D dissertation (University of Louisiana at Lafayette).

Doucet, Carol (2008) 'Une délégation du CMA bientôt en Louisiane: Les Acadiens du Nord invitent les Acadiens du Sud', CMA 2009 chronicle no. 12, 14 April.

Louder, Dean and Eric Waddell (eds.) (1983) *Du continent perdu à l'archipel retrouvé* (Québec: Presses Universitaires de Laval).

Reed, Revon (1976) *Lache pas la patate* (Montréal: Parti Pris).

Roy, Michel (1978) *L'Acadie perdue* (Montréal: Éditions Québec/Amérique).

6

FRENCH NORTH AMERICA: A JOURNEY THROUGH THE BIBLIOTHEQUE ET ARCHIVES NATIONALES DU QUEBEC ... AND OTHER INTERESTING AVENUES

Lise Bissonnette

One of the best ways of exploring how French North America came into being, albeit taking the opportunity to make numerous detours along the way, is to visit the Bibliothèque et Archives nationales du Québec (BAnQ). The collections gather together Québec's published and archival documentary heritage but, as many readers of this book probably already know and use them regularly, I wish to focus particularly on developments that are beginning to give new life to these resources and pull them out of relative obscurity. As a result they can now be offered, with unprecedented transparency, to a much wider and culturally diverse audience.

When it comes to using the new technologies to enhance access to knowledge and culture, BAnQ, despite its relatively modest size, is in the vanguard, as much for the services it offers as for the role it plays within budding networks, which are fast changing the nature of both scholarly and amateur research. This has led me to think about the documentary collections devoted to French North America all over the world and to ask whether the time has come, thanks to digitisation and networking, to make of that French North America a real, signposted, identifiable area in the immensity of virtual space.

My chapter is therefore divided into two sections:

(1) A brief, and non-exhaustive, look at the current state of the relevant collections, from the largest down to the smallest.

(2) A series of questions, rather than affirmations, about the conditions required to develop a new coherence between these collections, should this be desired.

I

By way of preparation, I asked our experts to provide a variety of inventories of our collections of published and unpublished documents plus those of other institutions we are already aware of, or that we can easily find on the Internet. We focused on the French presence in North America from 1534 to 1763, according to recognised and generally accepted landmark events, namely, Jacques Cartier's first expedition to the New World and the transfer of power over New France to Great Britain. Admittedly, a number of collections choose a later cut-off date (the cession of Louisiana comes to mind), but I would stress that this enterprise involves a certain amount of approximation and that the main goal is to illustrate a problem. The territories covered are, roughly, Acadia, Louisiana, New France and Western Canada.

The collections

This section is divided into three groups:

- Large institutional collections (in national or heritage libraries, archives, museums or universities).
- Small, dispersed collections (in regional archives, religious archives or historical societies).
- Cyber-collections.

Once again, the goal is not to list everything these collections contain, but to give an idea of how this documentary wealth is distributed among an infinity of dispersed sources.

Large collections

BAnQ's central mission is the most demanding with regard to such corpora, providing:

- 1,600 archival fonds from the period, divided among five repositories in Québec's major cities. There are treasures like the Fonds du Conseil Souverain (1663–1760), the Fonds Intendants (1626–1760), the Fonds Grands Voyers (1667–1915, and the fonds of a number of large families (such as Chaussegros de Léry, Bégon).

- In the area of published documents, close to 500 early books (printed outside New France until 1763), including very beautiful items relating to the discovery of North America. There are also about a hundred maps, some of which were displayed in our exhibition, *Ils ont cartographié l'Amérique*, held 26 February–24 August 2008,[7] and an exquisite set of period prints, mostly views of Montréal and Québec City.

7   This was our major contribution to the 400th anniversary celebrations of the French presence in North America. See www.banq.qc.ca/collections/cartes_plans/exposition/index. html

- Gradual online uploading. I will come back to this later when I take up cyber-collections.

Library and Archives Canada has close to 7,000 archival documents divided among 243 fonds and collections. Some are very prestigious including those of: the Compagnie de la Nouvelle France; the Ramezay, Chartier de Lotbinière and Beauharnois families; and a number of large, very important seigneuries (this information was obtained from the website, since LAC has not provided a description of its holdings from this period). We can assume there are greater riches than meet the eye on the LAC portal, particularly when it comes to published documents.

We do not have an inventory of collections at the **Bibliothèque Nationale de France**, so I cannot give precise numbers, but we know there are documents regarding New France and French America in at least seven departments: Eastern manuscripts; Western manuscripts; philosophy, history and social sciences; prints and photographs; the rare books reserve; maps and plans; and the collections of the navy hydrographic service.

The **Archives Nationales de France** and **Archives Nationales d'Outre-Mer** contain at least 25,000 documents on New France, not to mention what lies in the archives of the ministry of foreign affairs and the historical services of the army and the navy.

We cannot but envy the **British Library** for its collection of French Canadian imprints from 1764 to 1990, of which a two-volume catalogue was compiled jointly with the Bibliothèque Nationale du Québec in 1992–3. **The National Archives** of the United Kingdom's catalogue lists no fewer than 2,812 results for New France up to 1764, including Colonial Office, War Office and Foreign Office and State Paper Office records up to 1782, as well as a great many maps.

The **Library of Congress** is, of course, a particularly rich source (and so big that it ignored our requests for information …). There are references to New France in the Geography and Map Division, Prints and Photographs, the Rare Book and Special Collections Division, and various specialised collections (Margry, Rochambeau, Kislak).

Since these are large libraries, I was unable to obtain precise lists in time for when I delivered the conference paper upon which this chapter is based and my aim has remained simply to illustrate the diversity and size of major holdings relating to the French presence in North America and to point out that it is their good fortune, as it were, to be part of the largest documentary institutions in the world (**BnF, British Library and Library of Congress**).

We were unable to make a list of museum collections, exhaustive online museum catalogues being a rarity, but our own Centre de référence de l'Amérique française attached to the **Musée de la Civilisation**, in Québec City is worth mentioning. It brings together the rich archives of the Séminaire de

Québec and a number of private fonds of illustrious figures (including that of priest/historian Noël Baillargeon concerning the Mississippi Valley). The **McCord Museum**, in Montréal, also deserves attention. It has a wealth of documents from great figures and families (such as McCord, Amherst, Murray), a strong collection of military documents dating back to 1710, the Seven Years War in North America Collection, a valuable James Wolfe Collection, and several fonds for large seigneuries.

University centres that have built significant holdings relating to the French presence in North America include: the Centre for Research on French Canadian Culture of the **University of Ottawa**; the Centre d'études acadiennes of the **Université de Moncton**; the Division des Archives of the **Université de Montréal**; the Rare Books Department of **McGill University**, which has gathered a number of private collections; and the Center for Louisiana Studies of the University of Louisiana in Lafayette.

Small collections

Here, I will mention just a few of the places where absorbing documents on the French presence can be found, some little known.

In Québec, small archives and historical societies, about 30 of which are accredited by **BAnQ,** sometimes have very interesting holdings, particularly regarding seigneuries and major families in the regions concerned. There is much to see in the **municipal archives** of the major centres (Montréal, Québec City) and in small cities (like Vaudreuil or St-Hyacinthe). The small repositories with the most to offer, however, are the **archives of religious communities** (Ursulines and Augustines in Québec City, the Séminaire de Nicolet, and the Évêché de Montréal). These include fonds, such as hospitals, schools and morals, which are particularly useful for the study of ways of life. And there are similar holdings in Acadia, Western Canada and Louisiana.

In France, the riches of **departmental archives** should certainly not be ignored. According to our research, documents dating from the days of New France can be found in the archives of over 30 departments, especially in Charente-Maritime, Gironde and Pyrénées-Atlantique — regions our ancestors hail from. Various **heritage libraries** also report interesting documents (we traced over 20 such libraries), and one cannot underestimate the importance of **regional heritage holdings** in certain French municipal libraries, which are not listed anywhere, for lack of funds and staff to take inventory.

Cyber-collections

I cannot guarantee the accuracy of my findings in this category, which has been born of digitisation and migration onto the Internet of large and small pieces of collections of published or archival material like those already mentioned. Broadly, these collections can be placed into two groups:

Virtual libraries and archives in traditional form, i.e. large-scale reference tools as exemplified by **BAnQ**'s digital collections. We systematically scan our published heritage on the basis of our catalogues and lists established by the *Dictionnaire des oeuvres littéraires du Québec* (DOLQ) and are scanning all of Québec's notarial archives up to 1907. More than 43,000 French Regime archival files in the Champlain project went online in 2004, as well as 120,000 images, and, aiming for exhaustive coverage, we are continuing to enrich this corpus. **Library and Archives Canada** has scanned the full text of the Jesuit *Relations* and the *Dictionary of Canadian Biography* and, with Archivia.Net, has built a database of private archives and colonial documents.

But these classic reference sites are outclassed in virtual space by a bewildering multitude of thematic projects — some of them collaborative efforts between institutions; others, solo efforts by organisations both great and small. Examples of major projects are:

- the **Bibliographie des relations France-Québec**, jointly conducted by **BAnQ** and the **BnF** for over ten years, which contains thousands of references and has just begun to digitise its most important items

- the **Canada-France Archives portal**, a collaboration between **AnF**, the former **Archives nationales du Québec** and **LAC**, which began its second phase of development in June 2008. The English subtitle is *On French Soil in America*

- the **Global Gateway** of the **Library of Congress**, which develops collections with several national libraries in the world and, with the BnF, offers a section entitled *France in America/La France en Amérique* in the form of a bilingual digital library

- **400 ans de présence française au Canada 1601–2004** (Société historique de Saint-Boniface, Université de Moncton, University of Ottawa)

It is only possible to list a selection of the vast number of small thematic projects that have sprung up everywhere now that the Web is regarded as the communication and educational tool par excellence. Many are **virtual exhibitions**, of which it is worth highlighting:

- *Tracing the History of New France* (**LAC**)

- *La Nouvelle France, ressources françaises*, a gallery of ethnological objects representing Aboriginal peoples, and *French Louisiana 1682–1803* (**French ministry of culture**)

- The *Avalon Project: Franco-American Diplomacy 1778–1843* (**Yale Law School**)

- *The Louisiana Purchase* (**State University of Louisiana**)

- *American Journeys, accounts of exploration from 1000 to 1800* (**Wisconsin Historical Society**)
- *Virtual Museum of New France* (**Canadian Museum of Civilization**, Ottawa)
- *Champlain in Acadia* (**Historica Foundation**)
- The *Champlain Society Digital Collection*, a site of 83 volumes (40,000 pages) on 300 years of exploration, from Champlain to Franklin
- *Les collectivités francophones et les Métis au coeur de l'Amérique* (**Société historique de Saint-Boniface**)
- *Adhémar*, **Groupe de recherches sur Montréal** databases
- *Le maître Guillaume*, covering major historical figures and aspects of daily life in bygone days in Acadia (**Université de Moncton**)
- *Inventaire des lieux de mémoire de la Nouvelle France* (launched by the **Commission franco-québécoise des lieux de mémoire communs**)

II

This incomplete and somewhat dizzying overview raises significant questions which I address below. There can be no doubt these attempts — whether great or small — to provide the public with access to hitherto inaccessible resources only reach a tiny number of those who might potentially be interested, even though the material is offered free of charge and most people have Internet access. It was particularly evident in 2008 — when hardly a day went by without the mass media, at least in Québec, highlighting some project or event linked to the 400th anniversary of the French presence in North America or the founding of Québec City — that many of the multifarious initiatives launched on the Web went practically unnoticed, despite being supported by considerable human and financial resources.

Do these sources of documentation need to be federated — to avoid inevitable duplication, for one thing, but principally to organise this immensely rich corpus, develop it in an orderly fashion, give it the visibility suited to its size and, as a result, truly make it exist? Our natural tendency, as researchers or heads of heritage institutions, would no doubt be to nod our agreement, as is demonstrated by the large number of ongoing collaborations and by our daily experiences at Bibliothèque et Archives nationales du Québec. We firmly believe in online development, not just for fun but because it supports, in a very concrete way in Québec, our mission of democratisation of culture.

Who should be in charge of coordinating efforts? When it comes to archives and artefacts, which are much more complex to organise and less commercially interesting than books, one can assume that even Google is not about to launch into a massive digitisation programme, particularly for a corpus like that of the French presence in North America. That leaves the major institutions, which, each in their own way, are currently engaged in federated projects with even larger corpora:

- Global Gateway, with the Library of Congress (an initiative mentioned earlier)

- the French-speaking network of national digital libraries (Réseau francophone des bibliothèques nationales numériques [RFBNN]) founded by the BnF, BAnQ, LAC, the Bibliothèque royale de Belgique, the Bibliothèque nationale de Suisse and the Bibliothèque nationale du Luxembourg, institutions joined by certain national libraries in African countries, according to how much they can afford

- the Canada project, which has been actively discussed for some three years and seeks to bring together research organisations and national institutions like LAC and BAnQ for the massive digitisation of documentary heritage

- our own Québec digitisation project, conducted in collaboration with the Société des musées québécois, which is drawing up a list of the digitisation efforts completed and in the pipeline in all Québec institutions (libraries, museums, universities, historical societies), with a view to coordinated action and eventually the creation of a national portal.

The involvement of the major institutions is of course as inevitable as it is necessary. But will it last? The funding that the Department of Canadian Heritage granted to sites relating to the French presence in North America, under its Canadian Culture Online Program, is likely to dry up, having been geared to a now-past one-time celebration, 'The 400th'. It is probable that the Library of Congress will not move on to the second phase of the France in America project with Global Gateway, taking into consideration the constant postponement of the second phase and the information gleaned from those concerned. The broadening of the RFBNN, in which BAnQ plays a key role — developing the prototype — will depend on investments from the Organisation internationale de la francophonie, now entering a period of financial housecleaning, and on the commitment of its founding members, which, one has to admit, is variable. Some smaller federated sites are now drifting into obsolescence for lack of input and updating and that sounds an alarm for the larger projects struggling to adopt sustainable modes of organisation.

If it is already difficult to take inventories in one's own territory, as we are now trying to do in Québec, how will we manage it on a multinational scale, given that the holdings are dispersed among a multitude of regional organisations, particularly in the US and even more so in France? And is there a need to stem the proliferation of tiny thematic sites and virtual exhibitions — we offer our fair share at BAnQ — which give great pleasure to those who build them but, having failed to attract an audience, do not survive on the Web, lost as they are in a monstrous worldwide supply? The large digital libraries, like the BnF's Gallica, have stopped organising materials by theme (travel accounts, for instance) and gone back to a virtual offering close to that of traditional catalogues, where 'customers' make their own choices from a list that is as exhaustive as possible. This is the option we have adopted at BAnQ, giving priority to the corpora most in demand, like press sources and notarial archives, to name but two.

What copyright problems could arise? Most of the digitisation now done by our institutions involves heritage materials — works and documents free of copyright. But recent commercial developments, in both Europe and North America, mean that the digitisation of copyrighted materials will soon no longer be blocked. All that remains is for publishers and authors to agree with virtual producers an economic model that suits them. Is it too early to start worrying about striking a balance that will preserve heritage digitisation? The major digitisation initiatives are more likely to obtain funding if they deal with contemporary works rather than old corpora. Although of course aimed at a large audience, they would mainly be of interest to academic or amateur researchers.

Finally, is it likely that the corpus devoted to the French presence in North America will, like others, become an extensive thematic grouping of momentary interest that will gradually lose its relevance as memories of the 400th anniversary celebrations fade and, consequently, interest from the public authorities which supported them? From now on, we would like all scholarly conferences with which Bibliothèque et Archives nationales du Québec is associated to include a component devoted to the work of librarians and archivists and the evolution of collections. University research communities make great use of our resources and it would be beneficial if they now went a notch further and took an interest in the future of collections, traditional and digital alike. Immense development is inevitable, thanks to the extraordinary means at our disposal — that's the good news. But will this exponential development take place in an organised manner or in complete chaos? Our generation knows little else but the chaos that accompanies revolution. Those who follow will inevitably demand clarity. It is already time to think about what comes next and to prepare our legacy.

INSTITUTE FOR THE STUDY OF THE
A M E R I C A S
UNIVERSITY OF LONDON · SCHOOL OF ADVANCED STUDY

The Institute for the Study of the Americas (ISA) promotes, coordinates and provides a focus for research and postgraduate teaching on the Americas – Canada, the USA, Latin America and the Caribbean – in the University of London.

The Institute was officially established in August 2004 as a result of a merger between the Institute of Latin American Studies and the Institute of United States Studies, both of which were formed in 1965.

The Institute publishes in the disciplines of history, politics, economics, sociology, anthropology, geography and environment, development, culture and literature, and on the countries and regions of Latin America, the United States, Canada and the Caribbean.

ISA runs an active programme of events – conferences, seminars, lectures and workshops – in order to facilitate national research on the Americas in the humanities and social sciences. It also offers a range of taught master's and research degrees, allowing wide-ranging multi-disciplinary, multi-country study or a focus on disciplines such as politics or globalisation and development for specific countries or regions.

Full details about the Institute's publications, events, postgraduate courses and other activities are available on the web at www.americas.sas.ac.uk.

Institute for the Study of the Americas
School of Advanced Study, University of London
Senate House, Malet Street, London WC1E 7HU

Tel 020 7862 8870, Fax 020 7862 8886, Email americas@sas.ac.uk
Web www.americas.sas.ac.uk

Recent and forthcoming titles in the ISA series:

Caribbean Literature After Independence: The Case of Earl Lovelace (2008)
edited by Bill Schwarz

The Political Economy of the Public Budget in the Americas (2008)
edited by Diego Sánchez-Ancochea & Iwan Morgan

Joaquim Nabuco, British Abolitionists and the End of Slavery in Brazil:
Correspondence 1880–1905 (2009)
edited with an introduction by Leslie Bethell & José Murilo de Carvalho

Contesting Clio's Craft: New Directions and Debates in Canadian
History (2009)
edited by Christopher Dummitt & Michael Dawson

World Crisis Effects on Social Security in Latin America and the Caribbean:
Lessons and Policies (2010)
Carmelo Meso-Lago

Caamaño in London: The Exile of a Latin American Revolutionary
(forthcoming)
Fred Halliday

The Contemporary Canadian Metropolis (forthcoming)
edited by Richard Dennis, Ceri Morgan and Stephen Shaw

Latin London: The Lives of Latin American Migrants in the Capital
(forthcoming)
Cathy McIlwaine

Breinigsville, PA USA
17 June 2010
240115BV00001B/6/P